BUYING BITCOIN WITHOUT LOSING YOUR MIND

Step-by-Step Guide for Beginners

Buying Bitcoin Without Loosing Your Mind

Warren T

Copyright © Warren T, 2024

Except for reviewers who can cite short sections in their reviews

"All rights of reproduction, adaptation and translation, in whole or in part, reserved for all countries. The publisher is the sole owner of the rights and responsible for the content of this book. »

"The Intellectual Property Code prohibits copies or reproductions intended for collective use. Any representation or reproduction in whole or in part made by any means whatsoever, without the consent of the author or his successors in title or successor in title, is unlawful and constitutes an infringement, under the terms of articles L.335-2 et seq. Intellectual property code".

TABLE OF CONTENTS

Disclaimer 5

CHAPTER 1
THE RAT RACE IS RIGGED

Trapped on the Hamster Wheel 8
Are You Working Hard 11
A Glimpse of Freedom 14

CHAPTER 2
BUSTING THE MYTHS

"It's Just a Fad!" Wrong 18
"Too Volatile! I'll Lose All My Money!" 21
"It's for Criminals!" 28

CHAPTER 3
THE RICH DAD, POOR DAD APPROACH

Learn From the Masters: 32
From Liability to Asset: 36
The Power of Compound Interest 41

CHAPTER 4
TAKING THE PLUNGE

Setting Up Your Crypto Wallet 46
Finding the Right Exchange 51
Making Your First Purchase 56

CHAPTER 5
BUILDING YOUR BITCOIN PORTFOLIO

Dollar-Cost Averaging 61
Diversification 65
Rebalancing Your Portfolio 69

CHAPTER 6
UNDERSTANDING THE TECH

Block chain Explained 74
Crypto Jargon Demystified 77
Security in the Digital Age 80

CHAPTER 7
RISK & REWARD

Understanding Volatility 86
Risk Management Strategies 90

Long-Term Focus 95

CHAPTER 8
BEYOND BUYING

Decentralized Finance (DeFi) 100
Non-Fungible Tokens (NFTs) 104
Smart Contracts 106

CHAPTER 9
ADVANCED STRATEGIES FOR SAVVY

Trading Techniques 110
Staking & Lending 113
Tokenization 116

CHAPTER 10
THE FUTURE OF BITCOIN

Disruption on the Horizon 120
Regulatory Landscape 123
Bitcoin Adoption 125

CHAPTER 11
COMMON PITFALLS TO AVOID

Scams & Phishing Attacks: 128
Security Breaches 130

Emotional Investing 132

CHAPTER 12
STAYING INFORMED

Crypto News & Media 135

Educational Resources 137

Building a Community 139

CHAPTER 13
BUILDING YOUR BITCOIN LEGACY

Integrating Bitcoin 142

Tax Implications 144

Estate Planning with Bitcoin 146

CHAPTER 14: CONCLUSION
TAKING CONTROL

A Final Word of Encouragement 149

CLOSING THOUGHTS 151

DISCLAIMER

Don't Buy Bitcoin on a whim: A Beginner's Guide to Finding Your Way Around the Exciting World of Crypto. Interested in Bitcoin but feeling exhausted by all the talk? This e-book can cure the fear of missing out (FOMO). You'll learn enough about Bitcoin and have the right tools to enter the world of Bitcoin without losing your mind. Forget the false promises of getting rich overnight. This guide is mostly about learning Bitcoin's basic ideas and how it might change how money works; what you'll learn: The basics of Bitcoin and block chain technology, explained in simple, easy-to-understand language. Safe and sound ways to buy and store Bitcoin. How to go about the Bitcoin market with caution and avoid common mistakes. Essential things you should know to avoid scams and keep your money safe. "Buying Bitcoin With out Losing Your Mind" gives you the information you need to make intelligent choices about this new technology. If you want to join the Bitcoin revolution but want to be careful and do your study first, this is the book you need to read.

CHAPTER 1

THE RAT RACE IS RIGGED

"Why You Need a New Escape Plan"

TRAPPED ON THE HAMSTER WHEEL

Have you ever experienced something like a hamster on a wheel? Day in and day out, running without end, but never really going anywhere? Another Monday is forcing you out of bed when you awaken to the loud sound of the alarm. Driven by a sickening feeling of dread and stale coffee, you hurry through the morning routine. Work is a tedious job where you constantly have to fight against deadlines and your employer. By the time you come home, you only want to fall asleep on the couch because you're so tired and emotionally spent. Weekends provide a brief respite, but even those priceless minutes of relaxation are clouded by the impending Monday.

You promise to use your leisure time to follow your passions and begin the project of your dreams. But eventually, those aspirations get pushed farther down the to-do list as exhaustion sets in or Netflix entices with its seductive song of mindless pleasure. This loop, this never-ending hamster wheel, seems unbreakable. Despite your best efforts and payment of debts, you never seem able to advance in life. Inflation eats away at every rise, and unforeseen expenses destabilize your finances. The prospect of financial security seems like a far-off paradise you could one day get at by pedaling more quickly. But is this all there is? It is a persistent question that nags in the back of your mind. Is this all there is to life?

The annoyance increases. People around you seem to be leading the kind of life you wish you had—they're exploring the world, pursuing their hobbies, and creating futures they're enthusiastic about. You doubt your decisions and wonder where you made a mistake. Did you make a poor professional choice? Have you made poor financial choices? A simmering hatred towards your employer, work, and system begins. You get the impression that the cards are stacked against you. The fact is, though, that you are not stuck. You are capable of escaping this never-ending cycle. It won't be simple. It will need guts, tenacity, and a readiness to push yourself outside your comfort zone. However, it is feasible. Recognizing your current circumstances and this cycle for what it is—a soul-crushing trap that is robbing you of joy and keeping you from realizing your full potential—is the first step toward action. Feelings of frustration, rage, and helplessness are okay to experience. These feelings indicate that you're prepared for a change. Taking charge is what comes next. Examine your choices. Investigate alternative employment choices, learn about financial literacy, and determine what tactics can lead to economic independence. There is a vast array of opportunities waiting to be discovered. Finding what genuinely thrills you and makes you feel alive may take some time and experimentation.

Getting off the hamster wheel is not about getting satisfaction right away. It's not a sprint; it's a marathon. There will be disappointments, periods of uncertainty, and instances when the old habits try to entice you back. But you'll get closer to creating a genuine life with every step you take and every obstacle you overcome. A life in which you are moving towards something, not merely sprinting. A life full of passion, purpose, and the thrilling independence of being in charge. It's time to get off your ass and start building an exciting future for yourself. You can alter your situation. Are you prepared to make the initial move?

ARE YOU WORKING HARD

"Or Working Broke?"

Have you ever felt like you were working so hard at work—putting in long hours and giving it your all—but your bank account was always on life support? You may be working hard, but the harsh truth is that you may be broke. There are some problems with how things have always been done at work. We are told that if we work hard and stay loyal to one company, we will move up the business ladder. What if that ladder is broken and leads nowhere but to more work? What if loyalty only goes one way, and companies quickly replace "too expensive" workers with younger, less expensive ones? Working hard is indeed only half the battle. Putting in the hours doesn't ensure financial security these days. Many people can't seem to get off the path they're on, where they must work hard to keep up. They are busy, but that doesn't mean they're working hard. They're going upstairs, leading nowhere, and getting tired instead of rich. Your bills take up every penny of your pay check, leaving you with nothing to save or spend. I often notice you are afraid of paying for things you didn't plan for because even a minor setback can mess up your funds. This is called the "Just One More" fallacy. You tell yourself that you'll finally get ahead if you work a few more hours and take on another job. It keeps getting farther away, though, and the tiredness keeps growing. You might get burned out and not have enough money if you follow this "hustle culture" way of thinking. The good things about your high-paying, high-stress job keep you there because you can't quit. But how much does it cost? Are you willing to give up your mental and physical health for a nice prison? If any of these things happen to you, it's time to change how you see things. It's not enough to work hard. You need to plan your work to reach your long-term cash goals. Put money into yourself—you are your most important asset. Learn new things to improve your skills and make yourself more valuable. Look for openings at the company you already work for, or look into new job paths that will help you grow. When getting paid, the more valuable you are, the more your skills will be in demand. Knowledge is indeed power. Find out how to make a budget, save money, and spend. Learn about the business system and how you can use it to your benefit. You can find a lot of information to help you get started online and in libraries. Money is not a boss; it's a tool. Learn how you usually spend your money. Keep track of your spending and income to find places to save money. Make a budget that puts saving and spending for the future at the top of the list. Don't forget that getting rich takes delayed gratification, not quick gratification. There are other ways to get financially stable besides a paycheck every week. Check out different ways to make extra money. Look into side jobs, online companies, and ways to make money without doing anything. Having more than one source of income can give you more power over your future and protect your finances. Being healthy is valuable. Do not let your desire for money wear you down. Put your mental and physical health first. Ensure you get enough sleep, eat well, and healthily deal with stress. A person who is burned out won't work as hard, and for long-term financial success, you need to keep your body and mind healthy.

It's essential to work hard, but that's not all you need to do. You can break the cycle of working broke by being smart with your money, putting your schooling first, and taking charge of your financial health. Remember that you deserve a life with meaning, joy, and safety in your finances. Stop working just to get paid and start working towards your goals.

A GLIMPSE OF FREEDOM

"Why Bitcoin Could Be Your Ticket Out"

Picture a world where you're not stuck in a job that makes you feel bad about yourself and where your financial future isn't controlled by a system that seems to be rigged against you. Picture a world where you have more power over your money, time, and future. This world might seem like a faraway paradise, but Bitcoin makes it more accurate than you think. Bitcoin isn't just a digital currency; it's also a new idea that could change how money works and give people more power. Traditional banking is a closed system that governments and banks run. They decide on fees, interest rates, and how you can get to your money. Bitcoin is based on a decentralized network, which means that no one organization controls it. You have the keys to your Bitcoin in a digital wallet, giving you complete control over your money. What pay raise did you get last year? It's likely that inflation already ate it up. Because of inflation, traditional currencies are constantly losing value. Bitcoin is a hedge against inflation because there are only so many. It should theoretically gain value over time, making it a possible long-term investment for your money. When sending or receiving money between countries, the old-fashioned banking method can be slow and expensive. Bitcoin trades are quick, safe, and don't cross borders. There aren't many fees to send money anywhere worldwide, which opens up many options. The rules that govern traditional banking systems can make them hard to understand. The block chain is a public log that keeps track of all Bitcoin transactions. It is an unchangeable record of all transactions. Bitcoin is a safe and reliable way to store and send money because it is open and can't be changed. Bitcoin is an object that changes value quickly, but this can also be a good thing. You might be able to get richer with Bitcoin if you know how the market works and use innovative investment methods. This doesn't mean it's a way to get rich quickly, but it provides a different way to make money besides the usual markets. Traditional banking methods don't work for millions of people around the world. Bitcoin is a way for everyone to get access to money. The Bitcoin network is open to anyone with a smartphone and internet connection. This makes it possible for people who couldn't get financial services before to do so.

There are risks with Bitcoin because it is still a new technology. The market is unstable, rules are changing, and security risks exist. However, if you learn about and use it wisely, Bitcoin can be valuable for taking charge of your financial future. Ethereum isn't a magic bullet, but it does offer a glimpse of freedom. The chance to build a future on your terms, not tied to the rules of the standard financial system. It's your chance to work towards your goals instead of just getting paid. If you want to take charge and see what new options exist, Bitcoin could be your way out.

CHAPTER 2

BUSTING THE MYTHS

"Separating Fact from Fiction About Bitcoin"

"IT'S JUST A FAD!" WRONG

"Understanding Bitcoin's History and Potential"

Have you ever heard someone make fun of Bitcoin, saying it's a trend that will soon disappear? At some point, you may have even questioned its validity. Take a moment to learn about Bitcoin's past and how it could change the world of finance before you dismiss it. Bitcoin didn't just appear out of thin air in the basement of a computer billionaire. People lost faith in standard banks during the 2008 financial crisis, where it all began. In 2009, an unknown person named Satoshi Nakamoto published a white paper describing a revolutionary idea: Bitcoin, a digital currency.

What makes Bitcoin different

"Decentralisation" means Bitcoin works on a decentralized network, different from traditional currencies run by states and banks. In other words, no one group runs it. The transactions are written down on the blockchain, a public ledger that anyone can view. This openness and lack of a single authority are significant changes from the old way of doing things. Bitcoin has a limited quantity of 21 million coins, while fiat currencies (money issued by the government) can be printed whenever the government wants. This is one of the main things that makes it valuable. If more people wish to use Bitcoin and the supply stays the same, the price might increase over time. Thanks to security and the block chain, Bitcoin transactions are very safe. Since each transaction is encrypted and put into a permanent record, it is almost impossible to fake or change. This high level of security is a big plus over regular internet shopping.

A wide range of users from all over the world have been drawn to these traits. People are interested in Bitcoin because many people worldwide can't use standard banking systems. Bitcoin gives them a different way to send and receive safe and easy money. Many of the first people to use Bitcoin see it as an investment that will pay off in the long run. It's a good choice because there isn't much of it, and it could cause problems in the financial industry. Traditional currencies lose value over time because of inflation. Bitcoin could be an excellent way to protect yourself from inflation because there are only so many of them. Its value could also rise over time. Is Bitcoin just a fad? We still don't know. Even though its value has changed a lot in its short past, block chain technology, which powers it, is becoming increasingly seen as having the power to change many industries.

Getting to Know the Risks

Putting money into Bitcoin comes with some risks. The market is volatile, and no one knows if it will be able to stay that way in the long run. Rules are changing, and there are security risks.

Learning about Bitcoin, spending carefully, and being aware of its possible pros and cons could make it an excellent chance for you. Now is your chance to be a part of a financial change, to break away from the old system's restrictions, and to make your future. When someone says Bitcoin is just a fad, remember that it's a cutting-edge technology with an exciting past that could change the world as we know it.

"TOO VOLATILE! I'LL LOSE ALL MY MONEY!"

"Strategies for Smart Bitcoin Investing"

The world's attention is on Bitcoin's meteoric rise, but its crazy price swings can be terrifying. There are headlines about overnight crashes, and your friends may tell you that it's a bad idea to do it. But don't be scared off by instability. Take a deep breath and think about this: Vulnerability is like a sword with two edges. It can cause significant losses but also offers a chance to make substantial gains. To avoid the risk and make intelligent investments in Bitcoin, follow these steps:

How to Understand Volatility

Let's face it: the price changes of Bitcoin can be terrifying. The next day, you think you've lost everything and feel like a genius. This level of risk is average for a new asset type that hasn't been tested much. Bitcoin is still getting started, while regular stocks have been around for a long time and are backed by well-known companies. Its price is highly affected by supply and demand. Since there isn't much supply and the number of users is growing, news, regulations, and investor sentiment can significantly affect the price.

Knowing vs. Being afraid

Our "fight or flight" reaction can be set off by volatility. It's easy to make bad choices when you're scared, like selling things in a panic. The very thing you want to avoid is this. Instead, what you know is your most powerful tool. Learn about Bitcoin's background, how the market works, and the technology that makes it possible (blockchain). You'll be less likely to choose based on fear when you know more.

Putting money away for the long-term

Bitcoin isn't a way to get rich quickly. It's an investment for the long term, so there are risks. If someone tells you they can help you become successful quickly, don't believe them. You should expect volatility, so get ready for ups and downs. For example, planting a seed takes time to grow into a robust and healthy plant. Pay attention to what could happen in the long term instead of letting short-term changes determine your actions.

This is Dollar-Cost Averaging (DCA)

Dollar-cost averaging (DCA) is a solid way to handle market volatility and slowly build your Bitcoin portfolio. Yo u don't spend a large sum all at once; instead, you make smaller investments regularly, at set times, no matter what the price is at the time. In this way, the cost of a Bitcoin will level off over time. When the price is low, you buy more; when it's high, you might buy less. This makes volatility less of an issue for your total investment.

It's important to diversify.

Do not put all your eggs in one basket. There are other cryptocurrencies besides Bitcoin, though Bitcoin may be the most well-known. To spread your risk, you might want to add other well-known cryptocurrencies to your crypto collection. But remember that diversity doesn't consistently lower risk the same way it does in traditional markets, even though the crypto market is very volatile.

Put money into things that you can afford to lose.

This is the most important thing to remember when investing. Don't put more money into an investment than you can afford to lose. Bitcoin is a valuable asset with a lot of danger. Take it as such. Set aside a certain amount of your business portfolio that you wouldn't be devastated to lose for Bitcoin.

Keep Up-to-Date, But Don't Bore

Knowing about Bitcoin stories and trends can be helpful, but don't let it take over your life. Checking prices all the time can be stressful and cause you to make hasty choices. Set aside time to study and research the market, and don't keep checking your portfolio every five minutes.

First Safety

Protecting your Bitcoin wealth is very important. Keep your Bitcoin in a safe wallet, preferably one that can be used without an internet connection. Be careful when you use an online bank or exchange that has been hacked before. They should never be given to other people. As with any other significant asset, you should take extra care to keep your Bitcoin safe.

Look Past the Price

Bitcoin's price is only one part of the story. Pay attention to the science behind it, how it could change the financial sector, and how cryptocurrency is being used worldwide. If you think Bitcoin will be valuable in the long run, short-term price changes won't scare you as much.

You're Not By Yourself

You may not have been in this area before, but a group of Bitcoin fans is out there. Connect with other investors in online groups and learn from what they've done. Having a support system can be very helpful when figuring out the complicated world of crypto.

Bitcoin: Not for the Weak

If you want to invest in Bitcoin, you must have a strong stomach and think about the long run. It's not for people who are easily scared. Get ready for crazy price changes and the mental ups and downs that come with them. If you have a clear plan, a little courage, and an eye on the long run, Bitcoin could be a great chance. This is your chance to be a part of a significant change in technology and finance, to add a new type of asset to your portfolio, and maybe even make a lot of money.

Don't forget that you are in charge of your business journey

Do not let fear stop you. Learn as much as possible about investing, devise a good plan, and spend wisely. Bitcoin can be unstable, but if you know what you're doing, you can get through it and maybe even hit your financial goals.

Pay attention to your investment thesis.

It was coming up with your reasons to believe in Bitcoin. Is it the limited supply, the chance that it will shake up traditional banking, or the fact that it is being used worldwide? A clear financial thesis will help you stay focused and grounded when the market increases.

Do not chase the pump:

Don't get excited about a quick price increase. Remember that after these rises, there are often corrections. Don't let FOMO (fear of losing out) stop you from investing.

Don't Be Scared to Sell

There will always be market downturns. Don't let fear control what you do. If you think Bitcoin will be valuable in the long run, look at market drops as chances to buy.

Wait your turn

It takes time to get rich. Don't think that Bitcoin will make you rich fast. Remember your long-term goals, be patient, and stick to your financial plan.

Bitcoin is a Technology That Shakes Things Up

Bitcoin has the power to change the way we think about money and finances. It's a cutting-edge technology that could change many fields besides banking.

The Future Has Not Been Written

What will happen to Bitcoin in the future? No one knows for sure. On the other hand, understanding the technology, the risks, and the possible benefits of Bitcoin will help you decide if it should be part of your trading portfolio.

Bitcoin is a new and exciting type of currency. When you deal with volatility with knowledge, discipline, and a long-term view, it might become a friend instead of an enemy. Do not let fear stop you. Look into your options, learn as much as possible, and take charge of your financial future.

"IT'S FOR CRIMINALS!"

"Debunking the Dark Web Stereotype: The Legitimate Uses of Bitcoin"

When people think of Bitcoin, they frequently think of mysterious figures hiding on the dark web. This is a common misconception. Although the anonymity of Bitcoin can indeed attract illegal activities, it is a flawed assumption to believe that this is the primary purpose for which it was designed. Bitcoin can be utilized for various legitimate purposes, benefiting individuals and organizations.

Let's begin by dispelling the myth and then proceed to investigate the several viable applications of Bitcoin.
Sending money across international borders using conventional channels may be time-consuming and costly. Banks impose significant fees, and the clearing time for transactions might be several days. Transactions with Bitcoin, on the other hand, are both quick and unrestricted by borders. Sending money to any location in the world with minimum fees and typically in a matter of minutes is possible. Freelancers, remote workers, and organizations that operate on a global scale will find this to be a completely transformative development. Across the globe, millions of people do not have access to conventional financial

arrangements. An alternative is provided by Bitcoin, which enables anyone to participate in the economy of the entire world. Using solutions based on Bitcoin, they can safely store their wealth, send and receive payments, and even construct credit records. All Bitcoin transactions are recorded on a distributed public ledger called the blockchain.

Consequently, this results in immutability and transparency, which makes it extremely difficult, if not impossible, to falsify or manipulate transactions. By doing so, organizations aiming to simplify their supply chains or trace goods from the point of origin to the consumer can benefit from this. As a result of inflation, traditional currencies frequently see a decline in value. Bitcoin provides a hedge against inflation due to the limited quantity of cryptocurrency. As a potential long-term store of value for your money, its worth should, in principle, improve with time, making it a possible investment opportunity. The Fifth Point When compared to more conventional payment methods, Bitcoin enables significantly smaller transactions. Because of this, online content creators, musicians, and artists can now take micropayments for their work, opening up new opportunities. In addition, it makes it easier to bring about new business models founded on micro-transactions.

Bitcoin gives users the ability to take charge of their financial situation.

In contrast to conventional banking institutions, you have the keys (figuratively) to your Bitcoin, which grants you complete control over your funds. By doing so, individuals can autonomously manage their financial matters and circumvent the constraints imposed by centralized systems. The block chain, the technology that underpins Bitcoin, is a remarkable discovery that has uses outside the realm of digital payments. By assuring data security and transparency, it has the potential to revolutionize various industries, including healthcare, voting systems, and supply chain management. It is essential to recognize that Bitcoin is a relatively new technology that faces some difficulties. Scalability, energy usage, and regulatory compliance are some of the issues that are still being worked on. On the other hand, its potential advantages cannot be denied.

Be careful not to be fooled by the hype; Bitcoin is not a panacea for all problems. Investment in this asset is fraught with danger because it is volatile. It is not only for criminals hiding out on the dark web. It is a real financial instrument that can shake up conventional structures and give consumers more power.

CHAPTER 3

THE RICH DAD, POOR DAD APPROACH
"To Bitcoin"

"Investing Like the Smart Money"

LEARN FROM THE MASTERS:

"Robert Kiyosaki's Financial Philosophy Applied to Bitcoin"

You may have encountered the name Robert Kiyosaki if you have ever spent any time exploring the realm of personal finance. His book, "Rich Dad Poor Dad," questioned conventional ideas about how money is created, and it struck a chord with millions of people. His financial philosophy can be unexpectedly relevant to understanding Bitcoin and its potential influence, as demonstrated in the following.

In the Rat Race, You Will Fall
Kiyosaki's central theme is straightforward: most people are caught in a "rat race," in which they are forced to trade their time for money in a system structured to keep them working for a wage. Even if they put forth much effort, pay taxes, and rack up debt, they never fully achieve financial independence. This idea strikes a chord with many people who cannot escape their professions and are trying to make ends meet.

Is Bitcoin a Means of Freeing Oneself?

The cryptocurrency known as Bitcoin, which can upset conventional financial systems, can be interpreted as a means of evading the rat race. Kiyosaki strongly emphasizes the distinction between assets, which are things that bring money into your possession, and liabilities, which are actions that take money away from your possession. A long-term asset, bitcoin, has the potential to increase in value over time, in contrast to other assets, such as a vehicle or a house, which tend to decrease in value over time. Access to your money is controlled by traditional banks, which also determine the fees and interest rates. You have complete control over your financial situation because Bitcoin is based on a decentralized network operating system. This is in line with the idea that Kiyosaki is trying to convey: one should overcome dependence on old institutions and achieve financial independence. As a result of inflation, traditional currencies see a decreasing value. As a result of its restricted supply, Bitcoin can potentially serve as a hedge against inflation. There is a principle that Kiyosaki emphasizes in the process of accumulating money, and that is the idea that its worth should improve over time, thereby protecting your purchasing power.

This is the beginning of the cash flow quadrant.

The "Cashflow Quadrant" developed by Kiyosaki divides the various sources of income into four distinct categories: the Employee (E), the Self-Employed (S), the Business Owner (B), and the Investor (I). Individuals now have a new opportunity to engage in the Investor Sector thanks to the introduction of Bitcoin. You can produce passive income and go closer to achieving financial independence if you make strategic investments in Bitcoin.

A word of caution is in order.

Although Bitcoin presents several exciting possibilities, it is essential to remember that Kiyosaki strongly focuses on taking sensible risks and educating oneself about finances. Because Bitcoin is a volatile asset, investing in it is dangerous. Be sure to familiarize yourself, understand the market, and only invest money you can afford to lose before you commit to anything.

Beyond the Financial Aspects

As Kiyosaki emphasizes, achieving financial independence is not solely about having a lot of money. Having the time and leisure to pursue your hobbies and live your life according to your terms is what it means to have this. Bitcoin's potential for long-term development might liberate you from the confines of a regular career, enabling you to concentrate on what matters. Bitcoin's growth could be exponential over time.

It is a tool that Bitcoin is. Because it is a tool, it can be utilized prudently or recklessly. You may be able to use Bitcoin to break free from the rat race and construct a path toward financial freedom if you adopt the economic concepts that Kiyosaki outlines, which include pursuing financial education, taking risks that are calculated, and concentrating on growing assets over the long run.

FROM LIABILITY TO ASSET:

"Shifting Your Mind set to See Bitcoin's Value"

For a moment, try to picture a world in which money is not merely a piece of paper or digital digits stored in account records. Imagine living in a world where you are liberated from the constraints of conventional financial systems and have increased control over your financial situation. With Bitcoin, this may sound like a romantic fantasy, but it is a vision closer than you think. The problem is that many people have a negative relationship with Bitcoin. The way they perceive it, it is a "fad" that is uncontrolled, volatile, and has no real value. What happens, however, if Bitcoin is not a liability but a potential asset just waiting to be found? Changing your mind set can help you see Bitcoin in a different light, and this is how it can do that:

In the Transition from Uncertainty to Opportunity

Undoubtedly, the fluctuations in the price of bitcoin can be frightening. Note, however, that volatility works in both directions. Even though it can potentially result in huge losses, it also offers the possibility of significant returns. Undoubtedly, Bitcoin may be a rollercoaster ride, but it also has the potential to be a springboard for the expansion of the financial system.

The Transition from Hype to Innovation

It is common for the media to focus on overnight price jumps or dramatic frauds when reporting about Bitcoin since they enjoy a good narrative. On the other hand, blockchain is a revolutionary technology underlying all the hype. Bitcoin is built on a distributed ledger technology known as a blockchain, which is secure and transparent. Bitcoin is the first company to do so in this field, and its technology can potentially disrupt a wide range of businesses, from the healthcare industry to the financial sector.

Changing from a decentralized to an unregulated system

Uncertainty can arise due to the absence of centralized regulation surrounding Bitcoin. Nevertheless, traditional financial institutions have a track record of insolvencies and crises. Decentralization is the process of removing control from a single entity, which allows you to regain control of the situation. You are the one who possesses (figuratively) the keys to your Bitcoin, which grants you complete control over your financial situation.

When it comes to long-term strategy, investments are following.

If you think about Bitcoin as a strategy to become wealthy quickly, you are setting yourself up for disappointment. Nevertheless, considering it as a plan for long-term investing can be a game-changer. Bitcoin's value may increase over time due to the limited supply of the cryptocurrency and its growing acceptance worldwide. Consider it a seed you plant; it will take some time to develop into a powerful and valuable asset.

From Speculation to Scarcity: What Comes Next?

The world's governments are continually printing traditional currencies, which results in inflation and reduced purchasing power of conventional currencies. Bitcoin provides a buffer against inflation and has a restricted number of 21 million coins currently in circulation. Theoretically, its value ought to expand as demand grows, which might safeguard your cash for longer.

The Transition from Scepticism to Education

The absence of comprehension is frequently the root cause of fear. Consider devoting some time to educating yourself about Bitcoin rather than dismissing it as something you would rather not comprehend. Educate yourself about the technology that underpins it, the possible advantages and disadvantages, and the functioning of the market. As you gain more knowledge, you will feel more secure in your ability to make well-informed decisions on Bitcoin's role in your overall financial strategy.

The process of shifting your mind set

When you view Bitcoin as a liability, you cannot escape the constraints of the conventional financial system. On the other hand, if you consider it a potential asset, you can access new opportunities. It is an opportunity to broaden your investment portfolio's scope, participate in a technology revolution, and possibly come closer to achieving greater financial independence.

A word of caution is in order.

Bitcoin is not a silver bullet. It is an intricate asset class with its own hazard set. Do your homework, only invest money you can afford to lose, and avoid getting swept up in the excitement of the market.

Embrace the Future

Bitcoin is a pioneering technology that has the potential to transform the way we think about money and finance. Although it is not yet widely used, Bitcoin is a technology that stands out from the crowd. You may be able to appreciate Bitcoin's fascinating opportunities better if you change your perspective from one of liability to one of asset. Therefore, the next time you hear someone disparage Bitcoin, keep in mind that it is not just digital money; instead, it is a potential gateway to a financial future that is safer, more transparent, and potentially more profitable.

THE POWER OF COMPOUND INTEREST

"How Bitcoin Can Grow Your Wealth Exponentially"

Think of a situation where your money continues to work for you even while you sleep. The phenomenon of compound interest, which Albert Einstein frequently called the "eighth wonder of the world," is responsible for this phenomenon. When applied to Bitcoin, this powerful principle can unlock exponential growth potential for your money.

Describe the concept of compound interest.
Let us dissect it in detail. As a general rule, compound interest can be seen as "interest on interest." You are not only getting interest on the initial investment you made, but you are also earning interest on the interest that has accumulated over time. The faster your money increases, the more frequently interest is compounded (daily, monthly, or annually), the more regularly it is compounded. A Pairing That Would Be Perfect for the Cryptocurrency World? The interest rates offered by traditional savings accounts are pretty low, and they hardly keep up with the inflation rate.

Consequently, this indicates that the purchase value of your money is decreasing over time. Although it is a volatile asset, Bitcoin has the potential to experience tremendous price growth over a longer time. When you combine this with compound interest, you have a recipe for the accumulation of substantial wealth that has the potential to explode.

The following is how it operates.

For example, you decide to put $1,000 into Bitcoin right now. If the value of Bitcoin were to increase by 10% every year for the next ten years, your initial investment of $1,000 would grow to around $2,593 if one were to assume this hypothetical scenario. Let's say that after ten years, you still haven't been able to pay out. As an alternative, you choose to reinvest your $2,593, which enables you to earn interest not just on your initial investment but also on the accumulated gains. Continuing with the same hypothetical yearly growth rate of 10%, your investment would reach around $10,778 after another ten years if you choose to continue with it. This is an example of the power of compound interest in action: the longer you hold and reinvest your Bitcoin, the quicker it increases exponentially.

Essential elements to take into account

The price of bitcoin is subject to considerable fluctuations. Despite the possibility of big profits, significant losses are also possible. It is a commitment to the long term. During extended periods, compound interest is most effective. Do not anticipate becoming wealthy overnight with Bitcoin. View it as an investment with a long-term horizon. Dollar-cost averaging, also known as DCA, is a wise method that can be used to manage volatility. It is recommended that rather than investing a large quantity all at once, you invest small amounts at regular intervals, regardless of the current price. With time, this will average out your cost per Bitcoin.

Beyond the Numbers

It is not enough to chase statistics regarding compound interest with Bitcoin. Establishing a solid financial foundation for the future is the goal here. The sooner you begin investing and utilizing compound interest, the higher the potential wealth accumulation you have throughout a more extended period. Accumulating money through Bitcoin over a while can provide you with increased control over your financial situation, which may ultimately result in economic independence and the capacity to pursue your aspirations. Bitcoin can be a significant addition to a diversified investment portfolio since it provides a hedge against inflation and exposure to a unique asset class. For this reason, Bitcoin can be considered a diversification strategy.

A double-edged sword

Compound interest works in both directions. Compounding your losses is another possibility if the value of Bitcoin falls. The importance of intelligent investing and maintaining a long-term view cannot be overstated.

Taking a Step Towards the Future

The combination of Bitcoin and compound interest poses a formidable threat to wealth accumulation. Even though inherent dangers are involved, grasping the potential rewards will assist you in making well-informed investment decisions.

To increase your wealth with Bitcoin, the most important thing you can do is educate yourself, invest responsibly, and use the power of compound interest. The following is not financial advice; before making any investments, you should always conduct your own independently. You can put yourself in a position to take advantage of the exciting opportunities that Bitcoin brings if you have a solid understanding of the potential of compound interest.

CHAPTER 4

TAKING THE PLUNGE

"A Beginner's Guide to Buying Your First Bitcoin"

SETTING UP YOUR CRYPTO WALLET

"Where to Securely Store Your Bitcoin"

You are very welcome! You have decided to put your money into Bitcoin and take the plunge. Now comes the most critical question: where do you keep the coins you have worked so hard to earn? Conversely, Bitcoin is a digital currency that cannot be stored in a drawer like regular currencies. To keep your Bitcoin safe, you will need a specialized tool known as a cryptocurrency wallet. However, Choosing the appropriate wallet can feel intimidating due to the abundance of accessible options. Don't worry; we'll explain the many kinds of wallets, as well as the benefits and drawbacks of each, to assist you in finding the wallet that best fits your Bitcoin requirements.

Acquiring Knowledge of Cryptocurrency Wallets

Bitcoin is not genuinely stored in a cryptocurrency wallet as a digital piggy bank would. It stores the private keys in its place, allowing you to access your Bitcoin on the blockchain, a public ledger that records all Bitcoin transactions. You might think of it as a key to a safe deposit box; if you do not have it, you cannot access your Bitcoin.

These are the two primary types of wallets.
Wallets for cryptocurrencies can be broken down into two primary categories: hot wallets and cold wallets. The level of convenience and safety that each provides varies from one another.

Hot Wallets

Users will find that hot wallets are the most convenient alternative. Software applications are available for download on various devices, including mobile devices, personal computers, and even web browsers at your disposal. Because of this, they are perfect for daily transactions, such as using Bitcoin to purchase a cup of coffee. This phrase, the fact that hot wallets are connected to the internet, makes it simple to access your Bitcoin and other digital currencies. While this connectedness does make them more vulnerable to hacking efforts, it also makes them more secure.

Notable Examples of Hot Wallets

Many cryptocurrency exchanges provide built-in wallets for their users, which allow them to keep their Bitcoins after they have been purchased on the site. On the other hand, these wallets are custodial, meaning the exchange is in charge of the private keys. If you want to increase security, you might think about moving your Bitcoin to a wallet that is not under your control. On your mobile device, you may save and manage your Bitcoin accounts with the help of these user-friendly applications. Ideal for transactions that occur while on the move; however, be aware of the potential security hazards linked with internet-connected devices.

The term "cold wallets."

When it comes to security, cold wallets are the best option. Offline storage of your private keys is provided by these hardware devices, which are entirely separate from the internet connectivity. The fact that they are nearly impossible to hack makes them an excellent choice for holding significant quantities of Bitcoin for an extended time. Accessibility is the cost that was paid in exchange for increased security. Transactions involving cold wallets can be slower and more complicated than those involving hot wallets.

Popular Cold Wallets

These are actual devices that are similar in appearance to USB drives. Because they provide the highest level of protection, they are an absolute must for Bitcoin investors serious about retaining large amounts. Some of the most well-known brands are Trezor and Ledger. The use of paper wallets, which are a low-tech alternative, involves printing out your private keys on a piece of paper. They are incredibly secure if stored correctly, yet they are susceptible to harm or loss.

How to Determine Which Wallet Is Best

When selecting a wallet, you should consider your needs and your level of comfort with risk. A hot wallet that is simple to use, such as a smartphone application, can be sufficient for you if you are beginning your Bitcoin investment with a modest amount. However, when your Bitcoin holdings increase, you should consider moving them to a cold wallet so that they may be stored for longer. In terms of security, a hardware wallet is the gold standard, and if you are an experienced investor with an extensive Bitcoin portfolio, you should consider that.

Protecting Your Cryptocurrency Wallet

Security is of the utmost importance, regardless of your selected wallet. Ensure that your wallets have strong, one-of-a-kind passwords, and enable two-factor authentication (2FA) whenever possible. Be wary of phishing scams: never give out your private keys to anyone. Many phishing scams are designed to fool you into divulging sensitive information. The best way to ensure the safety of your private keys is to back them up on a device that is not connected to the internet.

Accepting Responsibility for Your Bitcoin

By selecting the appropriate cryptocurrency wallet, you can exercise control over your Bitcoin and ensure the safety of your digital assets. You can make sure that your journey with Bitcoin is rewarding by first gaining an awareness of the various alternatives and then emphasizing security. Please remember that this is not financial advice, and before investing in any cryptocurrency, you should always conduct your research.

FINDING THE RIGHT EXCHANGE

"Platforms to Buy and Sell Bitcoin with Confidence"

So, you've decided to plunge and put your money into Bitcoin. However, before you can begin to construct your cryptocurrency portfolio, you will need to find a trustworthy platform on which you may buy and sell your coins. Due to the enormous number of cryptocurrency exchanges that are now available, selecting the appropriate one can feel like an intimidating task. Do not be concerned; we will walk you through the most critical aspects to consider when locating the ideal exchange for your Bitcoin requirements.

An Overview of the Exchange Ecosystem
Cryptocurrency exchanges serve as marketplaces where users may buy and sell Bitcoin and other cryptocurrencies with other users or directly with the exchange itself. Different kinds of investors are catered to by the fact that they provide a wide range of features, fees, and safety precautions.

How to Determine Who Will Be Your Exchange Champion

The importance of security cannot be overstated. Look for cryptocurrency exchanges with a proven track record of providing a high level of security, including features such as two-factor authentication (2FA), cold storage for customer cash, and regular security audits. The regulations that govern cryptocurrency exchanges differ from one individual nation to another. To guarantee a certain degree of consumer protection, selecting an exchange that functions inside a regulated framework is recommended. While some exchanges provide fundamental buy and sell options, others appeal to more experienced traders by providing advanced capabilities such as margin trading and order types. Pick an exchange that is suitable for your trading objectives and your current degree of expertise. Depending on the exchange, transaction costs can vary significantly from one another. Take into consideration the expenses associated with trading, withdrawal, and any deposit that may be related to the various payment options. When purchasing Bitcoin, not all exchanges support the same fiat currencies, which are currencies issued by the government. Ensure that the exchange is compatible with the payment method that you select. The importance of a user-friendly and straightforward interface cannot be overstated, particularly for novices. If you want to explore cryptocurrency, you should look for an exchange with a straightforward interface, simple navigation, and helpful materials.

The Most Commonly Used Exchange Options

Allow me to provide you with a starting point by providing you with a glance into some well-established exchanges:

With its user-friendly design and support for various payment methods, Coinbase is a popular option for those just starting in the cryptocurrency world. On the other hand, compared to other exchanges, it could have more expensive fees.

Kraken: The Kraken platform is well-known for its advanced trading tools and rigors security features, and it is designed to accommodate both novice and seasoned investors. Compared to Coinbase, it provides access to a more extensive selection of cryptocurrencies.

Gemini: Gemini, which strongly emphasizes security and regulation, is a good choice for individuals looking for a reliable platform. However, it concentrates on providing deep liquidity for Bitcoin and Ethereum, although it only offers a restricted variety of cryptocurrencies.

Binance: Binance is a leading global exchange that offers a diverse selection of cryptocurrencies, competitive fees, and the ability to trade with advanced features. On the other hand, beginners could find the enormous number of alternatives available intimidating.

Getting Past the Well-Known Names
Even if large exchanges provide a sense of confidence, other, more minor market participants still have a good reputation. Before entrusting any exchange with your hard-earned money, you should always ensure you perform your homework on that exchange.

Things to Take Into Account
To ensure they comply with rules, exchanges frequently require verification procedures, sometimes known as KYC (Know Your Customer). Be ready to present documents that can be used for identification. Take into consideration the various payment options that are available for purchasing Bitcoin on the exchange that you have selected. Some accept credit cards, bank transfers, and even peer-to-peer options. If you experience any problems while using the platform, it is essential to have a customer care team that is dependable and quick to respond.

Taking the Initial Step into Account

To get started in the exciting world of cryptocurrencies, you first need to locate the best Bitcoin exchange. You can confidently begin your journey with Bitcoin if you give security, user-friendliness, and features that align with your requirements the highest priority. Please remember that this is not financial advice and that you should always conduct extensive research before selecting an exchange.

MAKING YOUR FIRST PURCHASE

"Overcoming Fear and Taking Action with Your First Bitcoin"

You've taken a small step into the world of Bitcoin. Congratulations! You have come to an understanding of its possibilities, selected a safe wallet, and located a trustworthy exchange. The moment of truth has arrived: you are about to purchase your first Bitcoin. Because Bitcoin is a volatile asset and the entire process may appear intimidating, it is natural to have some anxiety. However, you need not be concerned since we will walk you through the procedures and address the usual issues that people have to enable you to take action confidently.

Recognizing and Overcoming the Fear Factor

Although the unknown can be frightening, it is crucial to remember that knowledge is power. Before you invest, you should educate yourself about Bitcoin, including the possible rewards and the associated risks. FOMO stands for "fear of missing out," There is no need to give in to the pressure of the hype and make hasty choices. Invest only what you can afford to lose, and consider the possible returns over the long run. The fluctuations in the price of Bitcoin can be very nerve-wracking. It is crucial to remember that this stability also offers the potential for significant rewards. You should think of it as a rollercoaster ride rather than a freefall.

Step-by-step instructions for making your first Bitcoin purchase are included in this guide.

1. Put money into your exchange account: Before purchasing Bitcoin, you need financial resources in your exchange account. Depending on the platform, deposits can be made using a bank transfer, credit card (be aware of any potential costs), or other payment methods. The majority of exchanges allow deposits to be made.

2. Make your way through the Order Book: Buy and sell orders for Bitcoin at various prices, which are displayed in an order book, which most exchanges display. You can buy Bitcoin at the current market price by placing a market order, or you can choose to place a limit order to determine the price you are ready to pay.

3. Place your order by clicking here: After you have selected the type of order and the quantity, you should recheck everything before clicking the confirm button. Congratulations, you have just stepped into the world of Bitcoin ownership for the very first time!

To ensure the safety of your Bitcoin, you should avoid leaving it on the exchange for extended periods. You should move it to your private cryptocurrency wallet as a precautionary measure.

When it comes to making it a wise investment

Take a step back before diving in. First, you should begin with a modest investment to become familiar with the procedure and the market before expanding your exposure. This is a very astute method for effectively handling volatility. It is recommended that rather than investing a large quantity all at once, you invest small amounts at regular intervals, regardless of the current price. Over time, this will average out your cost per Bitcoin. Bitcoin is a long-term risk investment. Don't expect to become wealthy overnight. Instead of viewing it as a scheme to become rich overnight, consider it a potential asset for future growth.

Beyond the first purchase

You are very welcome! You have completed your initial Bitcoin purchase from start to finish. Always keep in mind that this is just the beginning. You should continue to educate yourself about the bitcoin market, keep yourself updated about developments in the business, and adjust your plan as necessary.

Embrace the ride that lies ahead.
Investing in Bitcoin is thrilling, with its fair share of highs and lows. You can put yourself in a position to potentially benefit from the possibilities of this ground-breaking technology if you can overcome your first apprehension, take calculated moves, and focus on the long term. Please remember that this is not financial advice, and before investing in any cryptocurrency, you should always conduct your research. Nevertheless, if you use the appropriate strategy and have some bravery, you can turn your Bitcoin trip into a profitable one.

CHAPTER 5

BUILDING YOUR BITCOIN PORTFOLIO

" Strategies for Long-Term Growth"

DOLLAR-COST AVERAGING

"A Steady Approach to Investing"

The world of investing may be a place that is both exciting and daunting at the same time. It is expected to hear tales of people who become wealthy overnight, but the fear of market volatility frequently prevents us from going after our dreams. This is where Dollar-Cost Averaging (DCA) comes into play; it provides a method that is both strategic and perhaps less stressful for constructing your investment portfolio, mainly when dealing with volatile assets such as Bitcoin (although it is not restricted to Bitcoin!).

Describe the concept of dollar-cost averaging.
For example, if you were to sprinkle glitter along a parade route, you wouldn't just dump the entire bag at once, would you? DCA operates comparably. This is a method of investing in which you invest a predetermined sum of money into a specific asset (such as stocks, exchange-traded funds, or, yes, Bitcoin) at predetermined intervals, independent of the asset's current price.

Why do you choose DCA? Efforts Made to Eliminate the Uneven Ride

The stock and cryptocurrency markets are notorious for their fluctuations, which can be highs and lows. You can negotiate this volatility with the assistance of DCA, which averages out your cost per share over time. Your fixed investment will get you fewer shares when the market is functioning at a high level. Fear not, however! Your set amount will allow you to purchase more shares if the market drops. As a result, you will have the opportunity to profit from future price increases potentially.

What are the advantages of using dollar-cost averaging?

DCA eliminates the temptation to time the market, which is a famously tricky task. This results in a reduction in emotional investing. Maintaining adherence to your plan allows you to avoid making rash choices based on swings in the market. DCA is committed to conducting itself in a disciplined manner. You make consistent investments, which helps you develop a habit and improves your chances of achieving long-term financial success. Volatility can be a source of intense anxiety. Thanks to DCA, you can maintain your composure with the knowledge you continually add to your portfolio at various price points.

DCA in Action: An Example of Its Practical Application

Imagine that you have decided to put $100 into a particular stock every month.

After one month: The price of the stock is ten dollars. You purchase ten shares for one hundred or ten dollars for a hare.

The second month: This brings the price up to $15. Even if you continue to invest $100, you now only purchase 6.67 shares ($100 divided by $15 per share).

In the third month, the market experienced a decline, and the price dropped to $5. You get a good deal by purchasing 20 shares with your $100, which equals $100 divided by $5 per share.

By making repeated investments of a predetermined amount over time, you can acquire shares at varying price points, potentially allowing you to average your share cost.

The DCA is not a magic formula.

Although DCA is a powerful tool, it does not guarantee gains or eliminate risk, but market timing is still unpredictable. The trend of the market as a whole continues to be a factor. The benefits of DCA become more apparent throughout a more extended period. As a result, time commitment is essential. A crucial quality is patience. DCA is not a substitute for extensive study before investing in any asset.

Are you a good candidate for DCA?

Among the many investors, DCA is an attractive approach. It makes it easier to enter the market without the stress of finding the time when you should. DCA is primarily concerned with gradual and consistent growth over time. It does this by averaging your share cost, which will help you control volatility.

Embrace the DCA approach to simplify your investment process.

If you want to expand your investing portfolio in a practical and potentially less stressful method, you might consider using dollar-cost averaging. It is possible to navigate market swings with more peace of mind and potentially profit from long-term gain if you take a disciplined and consistent approach. While seeing a financial advisor for personalized guidance is best, DCA can be a valuable tool on your investment path.

DIVERSIFICATION

"Spreading Your Bets for Reduced Risk"

Picture going to a casino and putting all your chips on one number. It might be fun, but there's not much chance of winning. In the same way, putting all your money into one stock, bond, or coin puts you at a very high risk. This is where diversity comes in. It's the most important thing, and there's a good reason.

What does Diversification mean?

Diversification means putting your money into various asset types to lower the risk of your whole portfolio. It's like putting together a safety net. If one purchase doesn't do well, the others might be able to help make up for it.

Why Spread Out? The Meaning of "Don't Put All Your Eggs in One Basket"

The world of money is hard to predict. The value of an investment can change a lot when the economy goes down, problems happen in the business, or something unexpected happens. If you invest in various asset classes (stocks, bonds, real estate, etc.), you're not just relying on the performance of one area. If the tech business goes down, your portfolio might still be safe because of how well healthcare or consumer staples are doing. Diversification helps you keep your portfolio's risk-to-reward ratio in check. You can put money into assets that are likely to grow, like stocks, for possibly high returns, and investments that are more stable, like bonds, for stability and income. Knowing that your stock isn't too dependent on a single asset can be comforting. Even though there may still be volatility, diversification gives you more confidence to weather the storm.

How to Build a Balanced Portfolio: The Art of Diversification

Diversification can't be done in a way that works for everyone. Your financial goals, risk tolerance, and time horizon will all affect the best way to divide your assets. A diverse portfolio can include stocks, bonds, real estate, commodities, and even cryptocurrency (but only if you're careful). There is even more variety within each asset class. When you buy stocks, for instance, you can put your money into different industries (like tech, healthcare, etc.) or company types (big-cap, small-cap). Don't just stay in your own country. Putting money into foreign markets can help you spread out your investments even more and allow you to see how economies grow differently.

Tools for diversification: What You Need to Build a Balanced Portfolio

Mutual funds and exchange-traded funds (ETFs) are easy ways to diversify your investments because they already hold various assets. Measure funds follow a certain market measure. They offer multiple investments and may have lower fees than actively managed funds. These online tools or meetings with financial experts can help you figure out how to divide up your assets to fit your goals and risk tolerance.

Diversification is a process, not a goal.

Diversification is a process that never ends. You may need to change your asset allocation to keep your portfolio balanced as your financial goals and risk tolerance change over time. Check-in on your investments often and adjust as needed.

Trust the Power of Diversification

Diversification is one of the most essential rules for investment. You might be able to lower your risk, make your portfolio more balanced, and reach your long-term financial goals with more peace of mind if you share your money around among different types of assets. Don't forget that this is not financial advice. Before you invest, you should always do your study. But if you use diversification as your guide, you can feel safer in the financial world and maybe even improve your future financially.

REBALANCING YOUR PORTFOLIO

"Maintaining Your Investment Strategy"

Think of planning your investments like following a recipe. You carefully pick the proper amounts of each ingredient (asset classes) to make a tasty and balanced dish (your financial goals). What will happen if you don't touch that dish for years? The tastes could shift, and the balance could become off. This is where rebalancing your portfolio comes in. This is an essential part of sticking to your investment plan over time.

What does "Portfolio Rebalancing" mean?

Rebalancing means changing your portfolio's asset mix to the percentages you set as your original goals. As markets change, so will the value of the different things you own. For instance, if the stock market has a great year, your stock investment could grow to be a much more significant part of your portfolio than you had planned.

Why Rebalance Now? Keeping the taste of the recipe

Your starting asset allocation shows how much risk you are willing to take. If you don't deal with it, a significant change in one way (more stocks, fewer bonds) can change your risk profile. Rebalancing your wealth ensures it stays in line with your long-term goals. An extensive stock portfolio might be good for growth, but it's not what you want if you're getting close to retirement and need more security. When you rebalance, you have to step back and look at your portfolio carefully. It keeps people from making emotional financial choices based on market trends.

How Often Should You Rebalance?

If the market is more volatile, you may need to rebalance more often (every year or so) to keep your goal allocation. More extensive portfolios may be able to handle a little more change before they need to be rebalanced compared to smaller ones. In the end, how often you rebalance relies on how well you can handle changes in the market. Some people like to rebalance once a year, while others might be fine with a broader range.

Rebalancing Strategies

Rebalancing can be done in two main ways:

Rebalancing based on a calendar means looking over your stock and rebalancing it at set times, even if the market changes.

Rebalancing Based on Triggers: Rebalancing is only done with this method when your asset allocation is off by a certain amount, like 5% or 10%. Sometimes, rebalancing can be done without selling. Selling assets isn't always a part of rebalancing.

Add New Investments: Instead of selling, carefully add new investment funds to your underweight asset classes to bring them back into line.

"Dividend Reinvestment:" Means putting returns from stocks or ETFs back into the same asset class. This lets it grow naturally.

Why Discipline Is Important

Rebalancing may not be the most fun thing to do with your investments, but it's necessary for long-term success. You were following your plan for adjusting, which shows that you are disciplined and helps you keep your eye on your long-term financial goals.

Rebalancing is integral to sticking to your spending plan and reaching your financial goals. By reviewing your portfolio often and adjusting it as needed, you can ensure that your investments stay in line with how much risk you are willing to take and keep your long-term financial plan on track. Don't forget that this is not financial advice. Before you invest, you should always do your study. But if you promise to rebalance, you can handle the constantly changing market with more trust and maybe even improve your financial future.

CHAPTER 6

UNDERSTANDING THE TECH

"Demystifying Block chain and Crypto Terminology"

BLOCKCHAIN EXPLAINED

"The Unbreakable Ledger Behind Bitcoin"

Imagine having access to a massive public Google Doc, but it is for transactions. This document is not managed by a single individual or organization but rather by a network of computers in different parts of the world. Within blockchain technology, this document is called a "ledger." The ownership of digital assets such as Bitcoin may be traced using this particular ledger, which was developed primarily for that purpose.

In the case of Bitcoin, the process is as follows:

Transactions: The block chain ledger is updated whenever a Bitcoin transaction takes place, which means that if someone buys or sells Bitcoin, the transaction is recorded.

Blocks and Chains: These transactions are collected together in what are known as "blocks," and these blocks are chained together chronologically to build a chain of information that is both secure and reliable. The acronym "Cryptography" Every block is cryptographically connected to the block that came before it, producing a chain that cannot be broken. If someone attempted to manipulate a block, they would have to manipulate all the blocks that came before it, which is arduous.

Advantages of Block chain Technology for Bitcoin

The blockchain has a high level of security because of its chained structure and cryptography, making it extremely difficult to hack or falsify transactions. Digital money such as Bitcoin must have this feature. All of the transactions that take place on the blockchain are visible to all of the users on the network, consequently producing a public and transparent record of ownership. A single corporation or organization does not control the blockchain. Because a decentralized network of computers manages it, there is no requirement for a central authority such as a bank to oversee its operations.

A Block chain That Extends Beyond Bitcoin

Blockchain technology can potentially revolutionize many industries besides cryptocurrencies, even though it has gained fame with Bitcoin. Track the movement of goods from their point

of origin to their final destination with increased transparency and security. Have the potential to create voting processes that are more secure and auditable.

Record Keeping: Securely stores sensitive documents such as medical records, land titles, and other sensitive documents.

The Prospects for Block chain Technology

Although blockchain technology is still in the process of development, it has a great deal of potential for the creation of a digital world that is more secure, transparent, and decentralized. There is a high probability that block chain technology will play a significant role in defining the future of finance and other areas of innovation as Bitcoin and other cryptocurrencies continue to flourish.

This is not advice regarding finances. If you are interested in gaining additional knowledge regarding Bitcoin or block chain technology, it is essential to conduct your investigation.

CRYPTO JARGON DEMYSTIFIED

"Understanding Common Cryptocurrency Terms"

Cryptocurrencies can be hard to understand because of many strange words and titles. Do not be afraid, brave customer! This guide will explain some of the most popular crypto terms, giving you the tools to get around in the exciting world of digital assets.

The Building Blocks
Picture a massive, public Google Doc where trades happen, protected by cryptography. This document keeps track of who owns digital goods like Bitcoin. Cryptocurrency is a digital form of money that is protected by cryptography. A well-known example is Bitcoin, but there are thousands more called "altcoins. A "wallet" is a digital device that stores your coin. It stores your secret keys, which let you get to your block chain coins. It's kind of like a safe place to store your digital things.

Business and Mining
Mining is making new bitcoins and ensuring that blockchain network events are correct. Miners use high-speed computers to answer hard math questions. The

person who gets them right gets new bitcoins as a prize. It's like gold digging, but it's in the digital world. You pay miners a small fee to add your Bitcoin transaction to the blockchain and ensure it is correct. A one-of-a-kind code on your cryptocurrency wallet that lets other people give you cryptocurrency. It's kind of like your public mailbox address. The private key is the most important part of your crypto wallet. It's like a robust password that lets you get to your coin. Do not let anyone else have your secret key.

Getting to Know the Market

Market Capitalisation (Market Cap) is the sum of all the values of all the coins in circulation in a cryptocurrency. For example, the sum of all the values of all Bitcoins in circulation. The government gives traditional currencies, such as USD, EUR, or JPY. The rate at which the price of a cryptocurrency changes quickly. Most of the time, cryptocurrencies are less stable than stocks. HODL is a typo that has become a crypto meme. It stands for "Hold On for Dear Life" and is a way to invest in cryptocurrencies for the long run.

It's essential to be safe.

Decentralization means that a cryptocurrency does not have a single body that controls it. A network of computers across the world checks and protects transactions. ICO stands for "Initial Coin Offering." This is a way for a new coin project to raise money by selling tokens to investors. Because ICOs can be risky, it's essential to study before investing—false attempts to steal your crypto by getting you to give up your private key. Be careful of emails, websites, or posts on social media that say it's easy to make crypto.

More Than the Basics

Any cryptocurrency that isn't Bitcoin is called an altcoin. There are a lot of different altcoins, and each one is used for other things. A stablecoin is a type of cryptocurrency that tries to tie its value to a stable asset, like the US dollar, to make it less volatile. Smart contracts that automatically carry out when certain conditions are met are saved on the blockchain, making it possible to trade digital assets.

This is not financial advice. This guide gives you the basic knowledge you need to navigate the exciting world of cryptocurrency. Before you put money into something, do your study, and never give anyone your private key. You can feel more confident about starting your crypto journey if you do some research and be careful.

SECURITY IN THE DIGITAL AGE
"Protecting Yourself from Crypto Hacks"

Cryptocurrencies have a lot of activity, but with that comes responsibility: keeping your valuable digital goods safe. Cryptocurrencies are used in the virtual world, which means they can be attacked online. Don't worry, investor who cares about safety! Here is a complete guide on strengthening your defenses and keeping yourself safe from crypto hacks.

The Dangerous Situation All the Time

Dishonest efforts come in the form of emails, texts, or social media posts from sources that look like they are real. They are trying to get you to give them your private key or click on dangerous links that can infect your device with malware and open your crypto wallet. When you use your crypto wallet or exchange, these harmful programs can get on your computer or phone and steal your login information or secret keys. Hackers get your phone number in this plan, which could let them get around the two-factor authentication (2FA) that some crypto exchanges and wallets use. Hackers can also go after cryptocurrency platforms, though this rarely happens. Because of this, it's crucial to pick exchanges that are well-protected.

Why You Should Build a Wall Around Your Crypto

You should always use strong, unique passwords when you can, and turn on two-factor verification (2FA) for all of your crypto wallets and platforms. This makes things safer by needing a code from your phone or another device in addition to your password to log in. Do not click on sketchy links or download files from senders you don't know. Check website addresses twice before you enter your login information. It's likely true if something seems too good to be true. Nobody should have your private key, not even "customer support." Companies that aren't scams will never ask for your secret key. Ensure the operating system and security tools are continuously updated on every device you use to access your crypto wallet or exchange. For extra safety, use a strong antivirus program and think about getting a hardware security key. Don't use your crypto wallet or exchange if you're on a public Wi-Fi network. Hackers will love these networks because they are not secure. Think about where you will put your cryptocurrency very carefully. For enormous amounts, you might want to think about a hardware wallet, a physical device that saves your private key away from the internet. A trustworthy hot wallet (software wallet) might be enough for smaller quantities, but ensure it has robust security features.

Knowing is power.

Keep up with the newest crypto security risks and the best ways to protect yourself. You can learn to stay safe at many trustworthy coin exchanges and wallet providers.

Why backups are important

It's essential to back up your crypto wallet like any other valuable item. In most wallets, you can make a backup seed phrase, which is a string of odd words that lets you get to your cryptocurrency. Keep this backup away from your computer, preferably in a locked safe.

Be Careful with Investment Tips

Be wary of people who say they can guarantee you a return on your investment or who tell you to invest right away without doing enough study. Before putting money into a cryptocurrency project, study it, and never put more money into it than you can afford to lose.

Cybersecurity dangers are constantly changing. You can protect your valuable digital assets and lower the risk of crypto hacks by following these security best practices, staying informed, and being alert. Do not forget that this is not financial advice. Before putting money into any cryptocurrency, you should always do your study. You can feel safer in the exciting world of crypto, though, if you take security into account.

CHAPTER 7

RISK & REWARD

"Navigating the Volatile World of Bitcoin"

UNDERSTANDING VOLATILITY

"Why Bitcoin Prices Fluctuate Wildly"

Bitcoin. Just hearing the name makes you think of prices going up and down dramatically, like on a financial roller coaster. Some people find this unpredictability exciting, while others find it scary. That being said, why does the price of Bitcoin change so much? Let's get ready to look into what makes these price changes happen.

Limited Stock, Big Dreams

Bitcoin's instability is caused mainly by how it was designed. Central banks can print as many traditional currencies as they want, but Bitcoin has a limited quantity. There will only ever be 21 million Bitcoins made. This lack of supply makes it possible for high demand to exceed supply, which drives prices up. The cost can fall just as quickly, though, if desire drops.

The Wild West of Rules

Cryptocurrency is still pretty new, and rules are still being worked out. Investors may feel unsure when there aren't clear rules and regulations. If there is good news about regulations, prices may go up. If there is terrible news, sudden selling may happen, and prices may decrease.

The News Cycle's Effect on Amplifying

The media loves a good story, and changes in the price of Bitcoin are great stories. Good news stories can make people want to buy even more, which drives up prices even more. On the other hand, bad news in the media can make people afraid, which can cause them to sell, which speeds up price drops. Remember that news stories aren't always the most important thing. It's essential to look at things in the big picture.

The Herd Mentality and Fear of Missing Out

Regarding money, feelings play a significant role, and cryptocurrency is no different. When the price of Bitcoin starts to go up, some buyers buy it right away out of fear of missing out (FOMO), which drives up the price even more. But if the trend changes, people may sell out of fear, which can set off a chain reaction that brings prices down.

The Coming of Age of a New Asset Class:

Compared to proven markets like stocks or bonds, cryptocurrency is still a new type of asset. Investors are still figuring out how much Bitcoin and other cryptocurrencies are worth, which can make the market more volatile. As the demand grows older, volatility is likely to go down over time.

What makes the market so speculative

Some buyers see Bitcoin as a risky investment that depends on what will happen. This kind of speculation can cause price changes. Some buyers hold on to Bitcoin for a long time, while others may buy and sell based on short-term price changes, which makes the market even more volatile.

How to Get Around on the Bitcoin Roller Coaster

Don't just spend without thinking. Learn about Bitcoin, blockchain technology, and the risks and benefits that might come with it. Markets are volatile. Only put money into investments that you can afford to lose. Don't get caught up in how prices change every day. Focus on your long-term investment plan if you think Bitcoin has a lot of promise in the future. DCA means spending a set amount of money regularly, no matter what the price is at the time. This might help the cost of a Bitcoin level out over time and lessen the effect of price changes. Always know what's happening in cryptocurrencies, but don't read every news story. The key is to take a fair view.

The price of Bitcoin is expected to keep going up and down for a while longer. However, instability should decrease as the market becomes more stable and rules change. You can feel more confident riding the Bitcoin roller coaster if you know what causes these price changes and use a well-rounded investment plan. Please note that this is not financial advice and that you should always do your study before putting money into any cryptocurrency. That being said, if you know a lot about fluctuation, you can make intelligent choices and maybe even get ahead in the future of Bitcoin.

RISK MANAGEMENT STRATEGIES

"Protecting Yourself from Downward Swings"

The world of cryptocurrencies is exciting, but prices can change quickly. Even though the chance of significant gains is appealing, the fear of sudden drops in value can be nerve-wracking. Do not be afraid, crypto explorer! Here is a set of risk management techniques that will help you get through the rough waters of the cryptocurrency market and maybe even protect you from the pain of big price drops.

Getting to Know Your Risk Tolerance

Step one is to learn more about yourself. How okay are you with the idea of losing money? Are you an adventurer who doesn't mind high risk and high return, or are you a cautious investor who wants stability? Figuring out how much risk you will take will help you make investment decisions and control your risk.

Spread out your crypto holdings.

Do not put all your eggs in one basket! Putting your money into many different cryptocurrencies can help lower your risk. Even though Bitcoin is the most well-known, there are thousands of other projects that are all different. To spread out your assets, learn about and pick cryptocurrencies that can be used for various things. But remember to only put money into projects that you fully understand after doing a lot of study.

Dollar-Cost Averaging (DCA) Saves the Day

DCA is a solid way to handle instability. You don't invest a large sum all at once; instead, you invest a set amount at regular times, no matter what the price is at the time. This method helps you find the long-term average cost per coin. If the price decreases, you can buy more coins for less money, which could pay off when the price goes back up.

Setting Your Limits for Stop-Loss Orders

Stop-loss orders are a safety net for markets likely to go down. Many coin exchanges offer them. You tell the exchange to sell your cryptocurrency instantly if the price drops below a certain level with a stop-loss order. This helps keep losses to a minimum if the market suddenly drops. But keep in mind that stop-loss orders can also cause sales that aren't necessary when prices temporarily drop.

Watch Out for Fear of Missing Out and Following Trends

Fear of missing out (FOMO) can be wrong in the crypto market. Don't buy a coin immediately because its price goes through the roof. Before investing, you should always research, learn about the project behind the coin, and consider how it might grow in the long run. It's the same when you follow trends. It's easy for hype to fade, and some projects may not be worth the trouble in the long run.

Put money into things that you can afford to lose.

Ten times as much of this golden rule applies to cryptocurrency. There is always a chance that you could lose all of your money in the market. Don't spend more than you can afford to lose without risking your financial health. Cryptocurrencies are a high-risk, high-reward business, so ensure you have a strong financial base before starting.

Keep up with the news, but don't rush to sell

Keeping up with the latest news and events in the Bitcoin space is very important. Do not let the sheer number of bad news stories overwhelm you. Changes are part of the game. It's not a good idea to sell quickly when the price of a project you believe in decreases. Pay attention to your long-term business plan and wait out the short-term drops.

Think about stablecoins as a temporary haven.

The value of a stable object, like the US dollar, is tied to the value of a stablecoin. They provide a short-term haven when the overall bitcoin market is very volatile. You can put your money in a stablecoin and wait for a good time to return to the market when the price is lower.

Don't forget that you're not alone.

For newbies, the crypto market can be too much to handle. You can find a lot of online communities and tools that can help you learn and get around in this space. Talk to people interested in cryptocurrencies, share your knowledge, and learn from each other's mistakes.

Management of risk is an ongoing process.

The crypto market is constantly changing, as should how you handle risk. As your portfolio and skills grow, you should consider how much risk you will take and adjust your strategies as needed. Remember that the goal is to keep you from losing a lot of money while still putting yourself in a situation where you may benefit from cryptocurrency.

Using these risk management tips, you can be more confident when trading on the cryptocurrency market and maybe even make it through the expected drops. Do not forget that this is not financial advice. Before putting money into any cryptocurrency, you should always do your study. With a well-rounded approach and a good dose of caution, you can find your way around the exciting crypto world and maybe even make it to a bright future.

LONG-TERM FOCUS

"Holding On for Bitcoin's Potential Growth"

Price changes can happen quickly in the world of Bitcoin. It's easy for investors to chase short-term gains or fear selling at the first sign of trouble when the news is about price spikes and drops. But for some, Bitcoin is a chance to make money over the long run and be a part of a technology that could change the world. If you want to invest in Bitcoin for a long time, here are some reasons you might want to hold on.

A Visionary Technology: The Possible Effects of Blockchain

Bitcoin isn't just digital money; blockchain technology makes it work. Blockchain is a decentralized ledger system that does not need a central authority to make deals safe and clear. This technology can change many fields, from healthcare and voting systems to finance and supply chain management. When you buy Bitcoin, you might not just buy a currency but also the future of blockchain technology.

Lack and Possible Demand

A crucial part of Bitcoin's creation is that there are only so many. In contrast to traditional currencies, which can be created endlessly, only 21 million Bitcoins will ever be mined. This lack of supply, rising knowledge worldwide, and the possibility of future adoption could make people want to buy Bitcoin in the long term. As long as demand exceeds supply, Bitcoin's price could increase significantly.

As a Guard Against Conventional Finance

There have been problems with traditional financial methods in the past. Bitcoin is an option because it is a decentralized currency. It's not run by a government or central bank, which could make it safer against inflation and unstable economies in traditional markets. A long-term investment portfolio might gain from having Bitcoin, even though it is volatile.

A Long Game Where Patience Helps You

You must be patient if you want to invest in Bitcoin in the long run. The market's prices can change a lot, and there will be times when they level off. Short-term hype and news cycles can cause a lot of instability. If you look at the big picture of what Bitcoin and blockchain technology can do in the future, you can get through these rough times.

Remember that past success doesn't always show what will happen in the future, so pay attention to the technology behind it and how it might affect things.

Putting together a strong base for the future
With DCA, you spend the same amount of money at regular times, no matter what the price is at the time. This method helps you better understand how much Bitcoin costs over time and might lessen the effect of price changes. Bitcoin is an investment with a lot of risk and profit. Don't spend more than you can afford to lose without risking your financial health. Think of Bitcoin as a long-term investment, and get your finances in order before you start. Bitcoin is only worth something if you can get to it. Keep your Bitcoin in a safe wallet. For more extensive amounts, a hardware wallet is best. Don't let anyone else have your secret key. Keeping up with the latest changes in the block chain and bitcoin space is very important. But don't let the daily changes in prices stress you out. Keep your eye on the big picture, and don't let short-term changes cloud your judgment.

Putting money away for the long term is like running a marathon. Putting money into Bitcoin for the long term is like running a race. Doubt and market changes will happen from time to time. There is, however, a way to possibly benefit from Bitcoin's growth over the long term. This is to focus on the potential of blockchain technology, use sound risk management strategies, and remain patient. Please note that this is not financial advice and that you should always do your study before putting money into any cryptocurrency. You can get around in the exciting world of Bitcoin and maybe even be a part of its future if you have a clear long-term plan and are patient.

CHAPTER 8

BEYOND BUYING

"Exploring the Potential of Bitcoin Applications"

DECENTRALIZED FINANCE (DEFI)

"A New Era of Financial Services"

Think about how money would work if there were no banks or brokers. A world where you have control over your money and can use peer-to-peer banking services. This is the big goal of Decentralised Finance (DeFi), a movement proliferating and using blockchain technology to change how money works.

Getting away from the old system

Financial institutions like banks usually control access to financial goods and services such as loans, investments, and trading. DeFi changes this model by making an open banking system that doesn't need permission to use. No bank checks or approvals are required to take part; anyone with an internet link can do so.

The Power of Blockchain

Blockchain technology is what makes DeFi work. It's also what makes Bitcoin and other coins work. A blockchain is a safe and open digital ledger that keeps track of all activities and can't be changed. This eliminates the need for a central authority and makes the DeFi environment more trustworthy.

A considerable number of defi applications

DeFi provides a wide range of financial services similar to and different from those traditionally available. Take a look into the world of DeFi:

Lending and Borrowing: DeFi platforms let users lend or borrow cryptocurrencies directly from each other, so they don't have to go through banks. This means borrowers may get higher interest rates on loans, and lenders may get lower interest rates on borrowers.

Decentralized Exchanges (DEXs): These are websites that let people trade cryptocurrencies with each other without using centralized exchanges. Users will have more control over their assets, and there may no longer be a chance of exchange hacks.

Farming Yield: In this method, people put cryptocurrencies in DeFi protocols in a planned way to get rewards or interest. But it's essential to know the risks before deciding to participate.

Decentralized Insurance (DInsurance): DeFi offers alternative insurance plans that use smart contracts (code that runs itself on the blockchain) to speed up the claims process and possibly lower costs.

The Possible Advantages of DeFi

DeFi could offer financial services to people who don't have access to traditional banks or don't have enough money in their accounts. Blockchain technology makes transactions clear and unchangeable, which could cut down on fraud and boost trust in the financial system. Because DeFi is open source, it encourages new ideas and quickly creates new financial products and services.

The Problems and Things to Think About with DeFi

The cryptocurrency market is naturally unstable, affecting the value of DeFi apps and user funds. Newcomers may find DeFi hard to understand because of the technical terms and changing standards. Studying a lot and ensuring you know is very important before joining. T

he rules and regulations that apply to DeFi are still evolving. Uncertainties can make it hard for adoption to spread.

Could DeFi be a look into the future of finance?

DeFi is still very new but can completely change how money works. We still don't know if it will be the future of banking or a significant force for change. But because it can give people more power and encourage new financial ideas, DeFi is a trend that you should keep an eye on.

This is not money advice. DeFi is sometimes hard to understand and dangerous. It's essential to study, know the risks and benefits, and only invest what you can afford to lose before jumping in. You can look into the world of DeFi and maybe be a part of this financial change if you are careful and know what you're doing.

NON-FUNGIBLE TOKENS (NFTS)

"Owning Digital Assets in a New Way"

There are many one-of-a-kind things in the digital world, from beautiful artwork to exclusive video game items. But how can you own something that's online? Non-fungible tokens (NFTs) are a new idea that is changing how we own and value digital assets. Imagine a digital trade card that is one of a kind. That's pretty much what an NFT is. A digital proof that proves ownership of an item and is kept on a blockchain (like the system that runs Bitcoin). Unlike regular digital files that are easy to copy, each NFT is unique and can't be replaced.

This makes a lot of exciting things possible.

Artists can now make one-of-a-kind digital works and sell them as NFTs. Collectors can buy these NFTs, which give them the original piece and the chance that its value will rise. Imagine having a unique sword that an NFT represents. In your favorite video game, NFTs could change how in-game economies work by letting players own virtual things and maybe even trade them. Things that used to be physical are now digital. NFTs can be used to buy event tickets, exclusive sports highlights, or even digital copies of collectibles that are real things.

Advantages of Having NFTs

NFTs are a safe and easy way to show that you own digital assets. Artists and other makers can make money directly from NFT sales. An NFT's value may rise over time, just like the value of any collectible.

Things to Think About Before You Jump in

There is a chance that the NFT market will go up and down because it is still new. As with any investment, you should learn as much as possible before buying. Some blockchain systems used for NFTs can use a lot of power. Look into eco-friendly options. An NFT's value is subjective and relies on things like the creator's reputation and the community's interest.

What's Next for NFTs?

NFTs are still changing, but it's clear that they have a lot of promise. They give you a new way to own digital things, value them, and connect with them. NFTs could be very important for the future of digital rights and the creator economy as the technology improves and rules are made.

This is not money advice. There are risks when you invest in NFTs. Study You can learn more about the exciting world of NFTs and maybe even join the digital ownership revolution if you are careful.

SMART CONTRACTS

"Automating Agreements with Blockchain Technology."

Imagine a world where contracts are carried out automatically, without lawyers, paperwork, or talks that go back and forth for hours. With the rise of intelligent contracts and self-executing programs stored on the blockchain, this futuristic idea is becoming a fact.

The Power of Code for Agreements

A smart contract is a code on a blockchain network like Ethereum. This code spells out the rules of a deal between two or more people. If certain conditions are met, the code will automatically carry out the contract, so there is no need for a third party.

As an example, here's a simple one

Let's say Bob wants to buy Alice's car. They can make a computer "smart contract" that holds the car's title. Once Bob pays the agreed-upon amount (in cryptocurrency), the intelligent contract gives Bob the title to the vehicle immediately. The blockchain does all this without needing a third party, like a bank. It is safe and transparent.

Smart contracts have these pros.

Smart contracts automate agreements, which saves time and resources compared to traditional paper contracts. Because they are stored on the blockchain, smart contracts can't be changed and are straightforward to everyone involved. Because smart contracts cut out intermediaries, they may be able to lower the costs of executing a standard contract. Smart contracts are automated and transparent, which can help people trust each other more when they sign a deal.

How Smart Contracts Are Used in the Real World

Keep track of where goods come from and how they reach their final destination with more security and transparency. Use smart contracts to automate claims processing and cut down on fraud. Make voting more secure and easy to check. Make it easier to buy and sell properties and manage ownership.

Things to Think About When Using Smart Contracts

The code that smart contracts are written in is what makes them safe. Unwanted results can happen because of bugs or security holes. Smart contracts work best for straightforward, simple deals right now. It can be hard to code complicated things. The laws and rules that govern intelligent contracts are still changing.

What's Next for Smart Contracts:

Smart contracts are a great new idea that could make many parts of our lives easier to do automatically. Smart contracts could significantly impact the future of trust and deals in the digital age as technology improves, laws change, and programmers write more complex code.

This is not money advice. It's hard to understand smart contracts. Even though they open up many exciting options, knowing the risks and limitations is essential before you use them. Intelligent contracts can open up a new era of automated agreements and make many parts of our digital exchanges easier if they are developed further and with care.

CHAPTER 9

ADVANCED STRATEGIES FOR SAVVY

"Bitcoin Investors"

TRADING TECHNIQUES

"Capturing Short-Term Gains in the Market"

The fast-paced world of bitcoin is tempting because it offers quick money. Long-term investing has its benefits, but some traders use active trading methods to make money in the short term. But before you start, keep this in mind: short-term trading is risky and needs skill, discipline, and a good dose of caution. Take a look at these strategies, but keep in mind that they are not financial advice. Before using any strategy, you should always do your study.

To read the tea leaves, do a technical analysis.

Technical analysis looks at past price charts and trading indicators to find good times to enter and leave a trade. Trying to guess how prices will move in the future by looking at patterns from the past is like reading tea leaves. In the past, the currency has either come back or been sold off in these price ranges. By finding these levels, you can start trades near support (to see prices rise) or exit trades near resistance (to see prices fall). These keep prices from going up and down too much, which could show trends. If the average goes up, it could mean that the trend is going up. If it goes down, it could mean the trend is going down.

"Trading Strategies for the Busy Trader"

Scalping: In this strategy, you make money from small price changes by joining and leaving trades quickly, sometimes in seconds or minutes. Focus, a good knowledge of technical analysis, and the ability to handle quick trades' emotional ups and downs are all needed for scalping.

Trading every day: Day traders get rid of all their trades before the market stops for the day. During the day, they might use different technical indicators to find chances.

These are just the beginning. Many other trading methods exist, and learning about and understanding each is essential before using real money.

Essential Tips for Trading in the Short-Term

Don't put a lot of money into it right away. Start with a small amount of money you can afford to lose, and slowly raise your investment as you get better. Set stop-loss orders to reduce your losses if the market goes against you. In the same way, when your plan works, don't resist the urge to hold on for more significant gains that might not come through. Instead, take your profits. The crypto market changes all the time. Stay current on news, rules, and project changes that could affect prices. Discipline is needed for short-term dealing. Follow your trade plan, don't make decisions based on fear or greed, and put risk management first.

Trading in the short term can be exciting and dangerous at the same time. Learn how to do it well, know the risks, and never put more money into it than you can afford to lose. Remember, there is no surefire way to get rich in the crypto market. For a more balanced approach to the exciting world of cryptocurrency, you should always do your study and put long-term investing first.

STAKING & LENDING

"Earning Passive Income with Your Bitcoin"

Not only can the value of your cryptocurrency go up over time, but there are also ways to make passive income with it. Staking and selling are two popular choices for people who own Bitcoin. Here are some ways you might be able to earn prizes without actually trading your Bitcoin.

Staking: Contributing to the network

Imagine getting interested in your Bitcoin to keep it. That's what staking is all about. You can stake cryptocurrencies that use a Proof-of-Stake (PoS) consensus method. Proof-of-Stake (PoS) differs from Proof-of-Work (PoW), which depends on miners solving complicated problems. PoS depends on validators putting up their cryptocurrency as collateral.

The process of staking

Users who lock up a certain amount of their coin to ensure that transactions on the network are actual are called "validators." Thanks to their work, validators get new cryptocurrency as a prize. The prizes you could win are more prominent if you bet more coins.

Putting up Bitcoin? Still not quite there

Since Bitcoin uses a Proof-of-Work method right now, it's impossible to stake it directly. A few platforms, though, offer "staking services" for Bitcoin. The catch is that these services often require you to give your Bitcoin to others, making the difference between staking and lending less clear (which is what we'll talk about next).

Putting your Bitcoin to work by lending it

Another way to make an idle income is to lend your Bitcoin. In traditional banking, it's like lending money, but no bank is in the middle. These sites put you, as an investor, in touch with people who need cryptocurrency. When you give your Bitcoin, you get paid back with interest, so you make money on the loan. Flexible or fixed terms? You can withdraw your Bitcoin at any time from some sites, while others have fixed terms that could have higher interest rates.

Things to Think About When Staking and Lending

Look into the platform's security steps before investing or lending your Bitcoin to ensure your assets are safe. Rates can change based on the platform, the cryptocurrency, and the terms picked. There is always a chance that the borrower won't pay back the loan. Some sites protect you from defaults, but the interest rates may be lower.

Staking and lending are fun ways to use your Bitcoin, and they can earn you money without you doing anything. But keep in mind that these are not risk-free activities. Before you stake or lend your cryptocurrency, you should always study, know the risks, and only use trustworthy platforms.

TOKENIZATION

"Investing in the Future of Digital Assets"

Think about a world where you could buy a small part of a Picasso picture, a house, or even a rare pair of sneakers right from your phone. Tokenization, a new idea that is changing how we think about and trade in assets, is making this futuristic vision a reality.

Breaking Up Ownership into Small Pieces

Tokenization means making digital tokens that represent ownership rights to a real-world object and putting them on a blockchain, which is the system that runs Bitcoin. It's kind of like slicing up a stock certificate. Investors can then buy and sell these digital tokens, which makes a lot of things possible.

Pros of Tokenization

Assets that were hard to sell before, like real estate or art, can now be broken up into smaller tokens that more people with less money can buy. Tokenized assets are easy to trade on digital markets, which could make them more liquid than traditional ways of owning things. Blockchain technology keeps a safe and transparent record of who owns what, which could cut down on fraud and make managing assets easier.

A Look at the Future of Tokens

Invest in a small part of a high-end apartment building or a commercial property. Fine art and collectibles: Own a piece of a Van Gogh or a rare baseball card without paying much money for the whole thing—private equity and venture capital: Access investment opportunities only open to wealthy people.

Essential Things to Think About

"Regulatory Landscape" means that the rules that govern tokenized assets are still changing. Before you invest, do some study. Tokenization doesn't eliminate risks; you must understand the underlying asset. Before investing, you should always learn about the object. Invest in tokenized assets through safe, well-known platforms that have been around for a while.

This is not financial advice. Tokenization is still in its early stages, but it can make investing more accessible to everyone and change how we own and trade assets. Before jumping in, you should study about the risks and benefits. If you are careful, you can discover the exciting world of tokenization and maybe even be a part of this new investing method.

CHAPTER 10

THE FUTURE OF BITCOIN

"Where Does the Road Lead?"

DISRUPTION ON THE HORIZON

"How Bitcoin Could Change the World"

The first and most well-known cryptocurrency, Bitcoin, is more than a digital currency. It's an experiment in technology that could change how we think about money and value. Even though Bitcoin's future is still unknown, here are some ways it might change the world:

"Financial Inclusion for the Unbanked"

A lot of people around the world can't use standard banking systems. Because Bitcoin doesn't need permission, it could give them a way to keep value, send and receive payments, and be a part of the global financial system without having to depend on banks.

There will be more openness and safety in the future.

Bitcoin events are written down on the blockchain, a public ledger. This makes the record clear and impossible to change. This could change fields like banking and supply chain management, which depend on trust and being able to be checked.

DeFi (decentralized finance) is on the rise.
The blockchain, the technology on which Bitcoin is based, makes DeFi possible. DeFi is a system of financial products and services that can be made without central banks. This could make banking services faster and more accessible for everyone.

A Threat to Traditional Currencies
Because Bitcoin is decentralized and there are only so many of them, it might be able to compete with fiat currencies controlled by states. Bitcoin might not soon become a common way to pay for things, but it could become a valuable asset like gold.

What the Future Holds for Work and Ownership
The growth of the blockchain could change how we work and what we own. Imagine a future where safe micropayments in Bitcoin make it easier for people to do unpaid work or where a blockchain records who owns digital assets.

Problems and unknowns that might come up
Price goes up and down a lot, which makes it a risky way to store value and a wrong way to pay for things in everyday life. The Bitcoin network has trouble handling many transactions at the moment, making it hard for many people to use. Governments worldwide are still figuring out how to hold Bitcoin, which could slow its growth.

We don't yet know how Bitcoin will change the world. But there's no denying that it has the power to change traditional banking systems, encourage new ideas, and give people more control. Don't forget that this is not business advice. It's hard to predict what will happen with Bitcoin. Before investing, you should always study and know the risks. If carefully thought out, Bitcoin could start a new era of financial inclusion, openness, and innovation, but it will be hard to become widely used.

REGULATORY LANDSCAPE

" Navigating the Evolving Laws of Crypto "
The world of cryptocurrency is new, exciting, and...uncertain. The rules that change all the time about how to buy, sell, and use cryptocurrencies are one of the things that people are most unsure about. Even though there are many different parts to the world scene, here is what you need to know:

Regulations that are all over the place:
In contrast to standard finance, where rules are already set, rules for cryptocurrencies are still being written. Some countries, like Singapore and Japan, have relatively straightforward and advanced regulations to encourage new ideas while lowering risks. Others, like China, have been stricter and made trading or mining cryptocurrencies illegal. The United States has complicated rules enforced by many different government organizations. This makes things uncertain for investors and businesses.

Areas of Focus for Regulators
Regulators want to keep investors safe from scams, fraud, and the fact that cryptocurrencies are very volatile. Anti-Money Laundering (AML) and Cryptocurrencies can be used for illegal things, so regulators are working on KYC

(Know Your Customer) rules and AML/CFT measures to stop this. Governments are still figuring out how to charge taxes on holdings and cryptocurrency trades.

What Does This Mean for You?

The rules and regulations are constantly changing. Keep yourself up to date on what's going on in your area. When you buy or sell cryptocurrency, only use sites that follow the rules and put security first. The cryptocurrency asset class is complicated and changes a lot. Before you buy, you should know what the risks are.

The Future of Cryptocurrency Laws

Countries need to work together more and more to set up a clear and uniform set of rules for cryptocurrencies. Regulators must work hard to find the best mix between encouraging new ideas in the crypto space, keeping consumers safe, and reducing risks.

Even though the future of crypto laws hasn't been written yet, one thing is sure: to survive in the exciting but uncertain world of cryptocurrency, you must stay informed, use trustworthy platforms, and understand the risks. This is not money advice. Before putting money into any cryptocurrency, you should always do your study.

BITCOIN ADOPTION

"Will It Become Mainstream?"

Bitcoin can change the way money works. But will it ever be a common way to pay, like having cash or a credit card? It's like looking into a crystal ball: the answer isn't clear.

Blocks to Widespread Adoption

The price of Bitcoin goes up and down a lot, which makes it hard to use for daily purchases. It would not be ideal to buy coffee with Bitcoin today and find it worth twice as much tomorrow. There is a limit to how many transactions the Bitcoin network can handle every second. This working time can't be widely used. A significant change in how people use Bitcoin is needed for it to become famous. A digital currency needs to be easy for people to use and hold.

Signs of Interest Rising

Big players like corporations and investment banks are starting to play around with Bitcoin, which shows that more people know its potential. Some online stores and even real-life stores are now taking Bitcoin as payment. This isn't the case for them yet, but it's getting there. Problems with scalability are being worked on to make Bitcoin transfers faster and more efficient.

What Did They Say?

Bitcoin might become an expected cash, but only time will tell. Its ability to cause problems and that organizations are becoming more open to it suggests it's here to stay. Bitcoin will obviously affect the financial world, whether it becomes the future of money or a good way to store value.

CHAPTER 11

COMMON PITFALLS TO AVOID

"Protecting Yourself in the Crypto Market"

SCAMS & PHISHING ATTACKS:

"Recognizing and Avoiding Crypto Frauds"

Unfortunately, some bad people want to join the exciting world of cryptocurrency. Scammers and phishers wait online to exploit people who don't know what's happening. How to spot and stay away from these crypto scams:

Watch Out for These Red Flags

It's probably true that if something sounds too good to be true, it usually is. Watch out for people who promise you huge gains on your cryptocurrency investments. Trustworthy businesses don't give away free cryptocurrency for no reason. If someone makes you a deal like this, don't take it. It's probably a scam. Scammers often use a sense of urgency to get you to make a choice quickly. Before committing to an investment opportunity, you should always take your time and do some study. Be careful clicking on links or visiting websites from people you don't know. People who use phishing often try to get you to visit fake websites where they can steal your login information.

Keeping yourself safe from cryptocurrency scams

Before investing in a cryptocurrency or using a new site, learn a lot about its history and credibility. Ensure all your crypto accounts have strong, unique passwords, and turn on two-factor authentication for extra security. Never Share Private Information: Some people call them "master keys" because they are like the real keys to your crypto. Don't give them to anyone, not even "customer support" who seems helpful.

Being alert and noticing the warning signs can significantly lower your chances of falling for crypto scams and phishing attacks. If something seems fishy, it probably is. Before diving into the exciting but possibly dangerous world of cryptocurrency, you should always put safety first and do your study.

SECURITY BREACHES

"Keeping Your Bitcoin Safe from Hacks"

There is a lot of potential in cryptocurrencies, but there is also a lot of duty, especially regarding security. Bitcoin and other coins are digital assets; hackers can get into them like you do with your online bank account. Here's how to keep hackers from getting to your Bitcoin:

Keeping an eye on your Bitcoin fortress

Safe Wallets: Use a secure wallet to keep your Bitcoin. The best defense against online hackers is hardware wallets, which store your Bitcoin offline.

Two-factor authentication and strong passwords: Use strong, unique passwords for your cryptocurrency wallets and turn on two-factor security whenever you can. This adds an extra layer of protection to keep people from getting in without permission.

Beware of Phishing Attacks: Phishing emails and websites can get you to give out your secret keys or login information. Be wary of any messages you didn't ask for, and never give out private information.

Stay Up-to-Date: To fix bugs, ensure that your software and wallet apps always install the most recent security changes.

More Than the Basics

Spreading the Risk: If you want to lessen the damage of a breach, you might want to store your Bitcoin in multiple wallets. Like you would back up any other important data, you should back up your wallet data regularly. Don't use public Wi-Fi to access your crypto funds or do business. These networks may not be as safe.

By following these security tips, you can make it much less likely that someone will hack into your account and steal your Bitcoin. You are responsible for your coin. Doing these things can protect your Bitcoin from cyber dangers and keep it safe.

EMOTIONAL INVESTING

"Avoiding FOMO and Making Rational Decisions"

The business world can be like riding a roller coaster, with thrilling highs and possible heartbreaking lows. Emotional investing, especially the fear of missing out (FOMO), is one of the worst things new buyers can do. Don't let your feelings get in the way of making intelligent choices with your money.

FOMO is the enemy of good sense.

Fear of missing out, or FOMO, can make you make bad investment choices on the spur of the moment. Seeing other people make quick money or reading about prices going through the roof can make you want to join the crowd, even if you know there are risks.

How to Choose Smart Investments

Look into an asset, company, or idea thoroughly before investing money. Know what the risks and possible benefits are. Don't just follow the crowd. Make a long-term investment plan based on how much danger you are willing to take and your financial goals. Markets will always go up and down. Don't sell in a hurry because of changes in short-term prices. Believe what you've learned and stick to your investing plan. Consider how an investment will do in the long run, not just how much people talk about it. Investing your way to wealth is not a sprint but a journey. Don't expect to become rich fast.

You can avoid the problems that come with the fear of missing out (FOMO) and make wise investment choices that fit your financial plan if you stay informed, calm, and focused on your long-term goals.

CHAPTER 12

STAYING INFORMED

"Resources for Ongoing Learning and Success"

CRYPTO NEWS & MEDIA

"Staying Up-to-Date on Industry Developments"

It's quick in the world of cryptocurrencies. You need to know about the latest stories and events to get around in this constantly changing space. To stay ahead of the curve, here are some tips:

The Following Trustworthy Sources

Websites That Cover Cryptocurrency News: Several websites cover cryptocurrency news and offer in-depth research, breaking news, and market updates. Look for sites that have been around for a while and have a good reputation for accurate and fair reporting.

Blogs and publications in the industry: Many blogs and publications share helpful information from blockchain and bitcoin experts.

Be Careful with Social Media: You can keep up with crypto projects and people who have a lot of impact on social media sites like Twitter. But be careful of accounts that can't be trusted and too much hype.

Adding different kinds of information to your stream

Podcasts and YouTube Channels: Several podcasts and YouTube channels talk about cryptocurrency in-depth and offer educational material. This can help you learn or relax while you're on the go.

Conferences and Events: By attending events and workshops in your field, you can meet other fans, learn from experts, and get a first-hand look at the newest trends. It's essential to think critically. Don't believe everything you read or hear without question. Before buying, you should always check information from multiple sources and learn more about the market on your own.

If you follow these tips and make a list of trustworthy information sources, you can keep up with the latest news in the cryptocurrency industry and make smart choices about your crypto trip.

EDUCATIONAL RESOURCES

"Deepening Your Knowledge of Bitcoin"

To learn more about Bitcoin, you need to be hungry for information and have access to good sources. If you want to learn more about this digital phenomenon, here are some great choices to think about:

Online classes: Coursera, edX, and Udemy are just a few online sites offering basic and advanced courses on Bitcoin and blockchain technology. You can learn from experts in the field at your own pace in these classes, which often give you certifications when you're done.

Notes: Many Bitcoin books are suitable for newcomers and experienced users. To learn more about Bitcoin's economics, start with "The Bitcoin Standard" by Saifedean Ammous. To learn more about blockchain technology, read "The BlockChain Revolution" by Don Taps Cott and Alex Taps Cott.

Documents: Documentaries like "Banking on Bitcoin" and "The Bitcoin Revolution" give a deep look into the background, philosophy, and effects of Bitcoin. You can watch these films on websites that stream videos or let you share videos.

Listen to podcasts: "Bitcoin Audible," "The Bitcoin Standard Podcast," and "What Bitcoin Did" are just a few of the podcasts that have interviews with investors, developers, and leaders in the Bitcoin business. Podcasts cover much ground and come in many forms, so you'll find one that interests you.

Consistent involvement is the key to learning well. Set aside time every day or week to review these tools, and don't be afraid to go over ideas that seem hard the first time. The more you learn about Bitcoin, the more you'll understand how complicated it is and how useful it could be.

BUILDING A COMMUNITY

"Connecting with Other Bitcoin Investors"

People don't have to go through Bitcoin on their own. Many people are interested in Bitcoin and are eager to share their information, experiences, and maybe even memes. Sites like Bitcoin Talk and r/Bitcoin on Reddit are great places to discuss, argue, and ask questions about Bitcoin. You can find experienced users happy to answer your questions and new users having trouble finding their way around. Join Bitcoin-related Facebook groups or Telegram conversations. A lot of the time, these groups have live chats, educational meetings, and talks about current events and market trends. There are Bitcoin meetups in many places where users can talk about the technology, make connections, and learn from each other. You can find these groups near you on sites like Meetup.com. You can meet more Bitcoin experts, investors, and developers by attending workshops or gatherings in your field. These events allow people to learn, connect, and keep up with the latest developments.

Outside of the Platform

Open communication is essential to the Bitcoin group. Do not be afraid to ask questions, even if they seem simple. Someone else likely has the same question. As you learn more, share what you've learned with other people. The group grows when people share their thoughts. Maintain a good mood and helpful attitude in the neighborhood. Always keep in mind that we are all on this Bitcoin path together.

By being involved in these online and offline communities, you'll not only learn valuable things from Bitcoin investors with more experience, but you'll also make friends and build a support network in the exciting world of cryptocurrency.

CHAPTER 13

BUILDING YOUR BITCOIN LEGACY

"Planning for Your Financial Future"

INTEGRATING BITCOIN

"Into Your Financial Strategy"

There's no doubt that Bitcoin can change how money works, but how can you, as an individual, use it in your overall financial plan? Take a look at this breakdown:

Low Value, High Potential

The value of Bitcoin changes quickly. It's like an investment with a significant risk and a significant return. Small investments, like 1% to 5% of your total wealth, can help spread out your risk and give you the chance to make a lot of money, but remember that they can also lose you a lot of money. Spend only what you can stand to lose.

Long-Term Goals

Bitcoin is still very new. We don't know if it will work as a long-term savings account or a new type of money. Think about the big picture. You shouldn't think of Bitcoin as a way to get rich quickly. Instead, think of it as a possible investment for the future.

This is Dollar-Cost Averaging (DCA)

DCA means putting a set amount of money into Bitcoin daily, regardless of the price. This method helps the cost of a Bitcoin level out over time, which lessens the effect of changes in the market.

Safety is Very Important

You are in charge of your own Bitcoin, meaning you have the secret keys to your money. To keep your Bitcoin safe from hackers, buy a strong hardware wallet and use strong passwords and two-factor authentication.

Get professional help

You might want to talk to a licensed financial expert who knows about cryptocurrency. They can help you determine how much risk you are willing to take and whether Bitcoin fits your general financial goals.

Bitcoin is a new and complicated way to handle money. It's essential to study, know the risks, and add them slowly to your financial plan with a long-term view of high potential rewards and the expected volatility.

TAX IMPLICATIONS

"Understanding the Rules for Bitcoin Investments"

No matter what, Uncle Sam wants his share. Even though Bitcoin is cool, it changes the way taxes are calculated. Here is a quick list to help you figure out how your Bitcoin activities will affect your taxes:

Bitcoin is a property in the eyes of the IRS

The Internal Revenue Service (IRS) of the United States sees Bitcoin as property, like stocks or bonds. This means you must pay taxes on any gains or losses you make when you buy, sell, or trade Bitcoin.

Want to Make Money Selling Bitcoin? Pay Attention

You'll have to pay capital gains taxes if you sell Bitcoin for more than you paid. The exact rate is based on your tax bracket and whether you kept the Bitcoin for a short or long time.

Spending Bitcoin is also taxed.
You can buy a coffee or a new tool with Bitcoin. The IRS will see that as a sale, and any cash gains may be taxed. Keep track of these purchases so you can file your taxes correctly.

Keeping Track is Very Important
Keeping good records of all the Bitcoin you buy, sell, and trade is very important. Crypto companies might not always give you 1099 tax forms, so making your records will help you report everything correctly.

Get professional help if you want to
Tax rules can be hard to understand, especially regarding cryptocurrency. Talking to a tax expert who knows about cryptocurrency could help you ensure you're filing properly and paying the least tax possible.

Where you live can affect the tax laws and rules you must follow. For help with your specific case, you should always talk to a qualified tax professional. If you know how Bitcoin affects your taxes and keep good records, you can enjoy the fun world of Bitcoin without getting in trouble with the tax man.

ESTATE PLANNING WITH BITCOIN

"Ensuring a Smooth Transition for Your Heirs"

Bitcoin and other cryptocurrencies are fantastic for encouraging new ideas, but have you considered what will happen to your digital assets when you die? Planning your Bitcoin estate ahead will ensure that your heirs have a smooth transfer and avoid confusion. To get you started, here's a list:

It's essential to be honest

Tell your friends and family that you have Bitcoin and where you keep it. This could be a hardware wallet, a particular exchange, or even a tool that stores your coins in the cloud. Do not leave them to find wealth in the virtual world. Describe how to get to your Bitcoin, including secret keys, login information, or recovery phrases. Keep these instructions somewhere safe, but make sure your heirs can find them quickly.

Think about a safe way to store things.

Hardware wallets are the safest way to store Bitcoin, especially if you plan to keep it long. Make sure, though, that your heirs know how to use it to get to their fortune.

"Multiple Signatories" is an option. For extra safety, think about getting a wallet with multiple signatures or keys that need to be approved by more than one person. This can help keep people from getting in without permission.

Think Outside the Tech

Write down how to access your Bitcoin funds and include them in your will or trust. This ensures that your wishes are officially recorded and clarifies things during the probate process. If your heirs know little about Bitcoin or how to handle their estate, you might want to teach them the basics.

If you plan and follow these steps, you can ensure that your Bitcoin is easily transferred to the people you want to receive it. This will help you avoid unnecessary problems or lost assets during a tough time. There are different estate planning rules in each state. Talk to a lawyer who knows about cryptocurrency to ensure your plan is legal and aligned with your goals.

CHAPTER 14: CONCLUSION

TAKING CONTROL

"Shaping Your Destiny with Bitcoin"

A FINAL WORD OF ENCOURAGEMENT

"Why Bitcoin Can Be Your Ticket to Freedom"

Bitcoin can be scary because it's full of constantly changing technical terms and prices. But behind all the confusion is a revolution that could happen: a chance to gain more power over your financial future. Bitcoin makes it possible for people who don't have access to standard banking systems to become financially included. People can keep value, send and receive payments, and participate in the global economy without depending on banks. Values of traditional currencies can go down due to inflation, which makes them less valuable over time. Because there are only so many Bitcoins in circulation, they might be able to protect your funds from inflation. Bitcoin deals happen quickly, safely, and all over the world. You can send and receive money across borders without the restrictions and high fees that usually come with business across countries. Coins let you be your bank. You have complete power over your money because you have the private keys. This gives you the power to handle your money without depending on outside organizations. Bitcoin is still new, so we don't know what it can do in the future. But it's a significant change in the way finance works, and it gives us a look at a more decentralized and user-controlled financial system that's on the way.

Bitcoin is an attractive, hard-to-understand, and always-changing world. If you do it smartly, carefully, and with an eye toward the long run, you might be able to become financially free and take part in this technological revolution. Know the risks, do your homework, and never put more money into something than you can afford to lose. However, using Bitcoin correctly could lead to a future with more financial freedom and power.

CLOSING THOUGHTS

We've come to the end of our journey through the exciting world of Bitcoin. This digital shift can change how money works, give people more power, and upset the status quo. It can be scary to start with Bitcoin, but you can get around this exciting area if you know what you're doing and are careful. Don't forget that Bitcoin is a complicated and risky currency. Do your homework, understand the risks, and give your money a good home. Will Bitcoin become a common way to pay? Time will tell. But one thing is sure: Bitcoin has started a change and will have a considerable effect on the future of money. If you know about Bitcoin, you can be a better participant in the always-changing world of finance, even if you don't decide to buy. Are you ready to start your Bitcoin journey? You can make your choice. Don't forget that the best investment you can make is in yourself. Now, you're well on your way to figuring out the exciting and maybe even revolutionary world of Bitcoin.

www.ingramcontent.com/pod-product-compliance
Lightning Source LLC
Chambersburg PA
CBHW070244230526
45470CB00002B/480